SYNCHRONICITY

By the same author

Rebirthing: Freedom from your Past

with Ean Begg

In Search of the Holy Grail and the Precious Blood

On the Trail of Merlin

SYNCHRONICITY

THE PROMISE OF COINCIDENCE

BY DEIKE BEGG

CHIRON PUBLICATIONS
Wilmette, Illinois

Published by
Chiron Publications 2003
www.chironpublications.com

ISBN 1-888602-31-7

Printed in the United States of America

To my husband Ean

The realization of the Self also means a re-establishment of man as the microcosm, i.e., man's cosmic relatedness. Such realizations are frequently accompanied by synchronistic events.

C. G. JUNG

CONTENTS

CONTENTS

ACKNOWLEDGEMENTS

I want to express my gratitude to all those angels of inspiration who have made it possible, each in their own synchronistic way, for this book to come into being. In particular I want to say a big thank you to:

My friend and supporter Eileen Campbell for suggesting I should write this book; my commissioning editor Louise McNamara for her continuous support throughout; Elizabeth Hutchins, my editor, who so skilfully tied up loose ends and always asked the right questions; Andrew Anderson, for painstakingly reading every word of the manuscript, and whose input and suggestions have been of greater value than he will ever know; Connie Burchell and Senta Rich for their immense support, their phone calls and e-mails throughout the writing process; my dear and reliable friends Ann and Carlton Colcord, with whom I had fascinating conversations deep into the night and whose London residence became a generous sanctuary, especially during the final stages of writing;

Helen and Jessica Begg for providing fascinating examples; Louise Macdonnell and Maha Sarkis for reading some of the chapters early on and for their valuable and honest comments; Sarah and Richard Dening for introducing me to the idea that the universe 'flirts' with us;

Vanessa Anson for sharing so generously her life story; Diana Binks, who taps into the Otherworld without being aware of it; David Cairns, who has a psychic dog called Amore; Thomas Hemsley, CBE, who sings like an angel and got his wish; Clare Martin, a great ski companion, who demonstrated that when the time was 'ripe' there was no stopping her from pursuing her destiny; Carol and Tom Patzau, who were meant for one another long before they knew it, and who have been good friends and gracious hosts;

And finally, Ching and Chow, my two Korat cats, who always knew when I needed a break from writing and pawed my computer keyboard until I got the message and walked in the garden with them.

Thank you to all of you, for without your input I could never have given birth to this book.

INTRODUCTION

In the designs of Providence there are no coincidences.

POPE JOHN PAUL II

Time present and time past
Are both perhaps present in time future,
And time future contained in time past.

T. S. ELIOT

At one time or another most of us have experienced strange and inexplicable happenings: someone rings just when we're thinking of telephoning them; a letter arrives containing exactly the information we need that day; a book falls off the shelf, we open it and the words we read hit us right between the eyes; we find ourselves sitting next to someone on a train who turns out to be a vital catalyst for future events. How do such things happen and, more importantly, *why* do they happen and *what* are they for?

This process of 'synchronicity' is a puzzle that no one has so far been able to explain satisfactorily, though the majority of people today are familiar with the idea. When I began my research for this book I was astonished to find that an understanding of synchronicity is fundamental to a deeper and more profound experience of human existence. Furthermore, I realized that we can only speak of something happening 'synchronistically' if it is witnessed; in other words, if someone can testify that an outer event, such as a book falling off a shelf onto someone's head, coincides with an important piece of information contained therein, which that individual was in need of at the time.

One of the most famous examples of this is when an apple fell from a tree and hit Isaac Newton on the head. In an instant he had vital new insights into the physical properties of gravity. Similarly, when Archimedes got into an overfull bath, displacing the water over the edge, he shouted, 'Eureka!' because in that very moment he knew how to measure the volume of an object by water displacement.

The same principle is still at work today – and not just for scientists, but for all of us. The reason I have written this book is my growing realization that synchronicity has become a potent ordering principle in my life. It is as though the spirit of synchronicity grabbed me and said, 'After all we've been through together, isn't it the *right time* for you to acknowledge me?' I had to agree. What follows is therefore to a large extent an account of my own experiences playing time-tag with this puckish sprite, round and round the mulberry bush, in and out of ordinary common-sense reality.

Quite often synchronistic phenomena are announcements of important coming events; at other times they are signs of comfort, which assure us that 'all shall be well'. They can also be signposts that show us which way to go next, or which way *not* to go next. Again and again they give us the feeling that we are in contact with something that looks out for us, which has our own best interests at heart and which will be present whether we invoke it or not.

Our 'synchronistic sense' is more acute when we are away from our daily habits and customary environment, such as when we are travelling in foreign places with few signposts, or none at all. Our cognitive abilities are enhanced when in unknown surroundings and we need to rely more on instinct and intuition. I have found that some of the most astounding meaningful coincidences have happened to me in this way.

I believe that discerning whether a synchronistic event is telling us to take positive action or whether to wait or do nothing at all is the key to success. Sometimes the signals are loud and clear and a swift response is needed, at other times they can be confusing or vague. *How* we interpret the signs depends on how sensitive we are to the callings from a world that lies beyond our physical limits and how willing we are to change. It is my belief that we sometimes deliberately block out synchronistic occurrences in order not to go down the road that leads to greater independence and freedom. Some people are comforted by synchronicity, for it suggests to them that they are under the influence of divine guidance. Others are petrified, because to them it means that they are not in control – at any moment Fate could step in and deal them a nasty blow.

Frequently there are no indications at all that we have a choice about how we respond to a synchronistic event; we realize only later that an event *wanted* to happen, whether we had any say in it or not. An example of a positive response to the promptings of Fate will clarify what I mean. I was once returning to London from a work trip to Washington, DC, via New York. On each seat of the small commuter plane lay a scratch card with 12 circles on it. At first I ignored the card, as I am one of these people who never win anything. But just before we landed I had another look. The text informed me that beneath some circles was the name of a city to which you would win two return flights from your local airport. To play the game I had to scratch off one circle. I held the card in my left hand for a while and then passed my fingers over each circle in turn. As I passed over one particular circle I could feel a buzz in the tip of my right index finger. I didn't trust that, so I repeated the test, and lo and behold my finger buzzed again over the same circle. I scratched it off and found I had won a free trip for two to Mexico City! I thought that there must be a catch to this, so I put the card in my handbag to read the small print later. Then I remembered that a couple of years earlier I had dreamed that I was in Mexico City with my husband. It was an ancient city in the mountains, built on mud. I had never been there before and didn't know that Mexico City was indeed built on mud. Remembering this dream told me instantly that I would get those tickets. Back home no one believed that the prize was genuine, but I sent the card off anyway. It was six months before I heard anything, but then I received an unconditional offer from the airline.

My husband Ean and I were soon travelling through Mexico in a battered Volkswagen Beetle. We spent the last night in Cuernavaca, in a beautiful hotel that was once a monastery. The paradisiacal gardens, with their pools, exotic flowers and dark trees, were so entrancing that the following morning we made no haste in departing. Indeed, we went for another swim and then leisurely set off for Mexico City airport. We returned the hire car and as our plane for Houston, Texas, was not leaving till later that night, we made for the restaurant for a light snack.

As we waited for our meal I pulled out our tickets and absent-mindedly leafed through them. My eyes fixed on the space that said 'Depart' and the time which was printed next to it. 'I'm just going down to the ticket desk,' I said calmly, although my heart was beating like a hammer. 'There's something not quite right with our tickets.' There certainly was something quite wrong with our tickets. We had missed our plane and Ean was due to deliver a lecture in London in a couple of days' time.

When I finally managed to talk to someone about our dilemma ('traffic congestion' was my excuse) they offered us a choice of flights. We agreed to fly to Houston that evening, spend the night in the airport hotel and take the afternoon flight to London. The flight was uneventful except that I had no appetite and declined the in-flight meal. Around midnight we wheeled our luggage trolley into the huge bedroom with its two enormous beds and all mod cons, and shortly retired for the night.

At around 2.30 a.m. I awoke with severe stomach cramps and an urge to go to the bathroom. For the next hour or so I stayed there whilst 'Montezuma's revenge', a major form of dysentery common in Mexico, had its way with me. The next few hours were a nightmare because Ean woke soon after with the same curse and we had to take turns in occupying the bathroom. As soon as I was able, I cancelled the big Texan breakfast we had ordered and began to take homoeopathic remedies every two hours. By 10 a.m. we were relatively stable and we managed to rest until it was time to prepare for the flight home. Although still suffering from abdominal cramps, we felt confident enough to dare the onward journey. We were lucky because people have been known to suffer for weeks from this potentially life-threatening illness.

What has all this to do with synchronicity? Quite a lot, actually. Ean and I are seasoned travellers and are the authors of two travel guidebooks. Never before had we missed a plane or a train. So why had neither of us bothered to check the tickets? With hindsight, of course, we realized that 'something' was watching over us and had prevented us from taking the flight to London that night. Can you imagine starting with Montezuma's revenge on a full Jumbo Jet, with a limited amount of loos? It does not bear thinking about.

If someone had simply told us not to travel, we would have laughed and in any case would have found it too difficult to reschedule our flights, quite apart from the extra hotel expenses involved and the fact that we had to be back in London for the lecture. So this 'other intelligence' simply made us forget our tickets altogether.

The question that I kept mulling over in my head for a long time afterwards was: is it possible that there exists another 'self' that lives alongside the self we know and does this self know more than we do? Does this mean that the future is knowable? And if so, was our experience proof of this?

Synchronistic events frequently intervene to warn us if we are on the wrong path. In a curious way we find out that we are not at liberty to do as we wish with our lives. If we persist with dogged determination in going our own way and disregard signs to the contrary, we will sooner or later have to pay for our foolishness. This type of going against the grain is quite different from someone who *knows* in some uncanny way that they must pursue a particular route in the face of opposition in order to achieve a very specific and crucial aim. Becoming sensitive to what is 'shadowing' us is the key. Knowing when a sign is a warning, when it is a test and when it is an affirmation makes all the difference to whether we will negotiate life's endless challenges efficiently and with the least possible expenditure of energy, or whether we will drift this way and that, hoping for the best.

A few years ago we had arranged to give a lecture to a group of psychology students at the University of Barcelona as well as explore the possibility of going to live in the city. We had booked an early morning flight and drove to the airport in plenty of time, parked the car and made for the departure hall. But looking at the monitor we noticed that our flight wasn't on it. We were not puzzled for very long, because when I checked our tickets, we realized that we were at the wrong airport! We were at Gatwick, south of London, when we should have been at Luton, to the north. The distance between the two airports was more than an hour's drive. We were standing outside wondering what to do when a taxi driver came up to us and asked what the problem was. He suggested that if we wanted to catch that plane we'd better get into his car immediately as the morning rush hour would soon begin and then there would be no guarantee that we would make our flight. We could have driven ourselves, but that would have meant losing precious time collecting our car and parking it the other end. So we took the most expensive taxi ride ever and prayed. We did make the plane – in fact the computers were down at Luton airport that morning and we finally left after two hours' delay.

At the time we said that because we don't usually fly from Luton airport it was an easy enough mistake to make. But gradually a pattern emerged. Every time we went to Spain to look for property or to meet someone connected with our professions, a Spanish *desencuentro*, or 'non-meeting' happened. Someone wrote down her own telephone number wrongly and was not listed in the directory; we locked our car keys in the boot; people we were meant to meet suddenly disappeared. The most telling sign was when we locked ourselves out of the apartment we had rented – with the key in the lock on the inside! That really did it. We finally understood that we were not meant to live in Spain. We ended up in the opposite direction instead, in Scotland.

As you will see from this, synchronistic occurrences are not isolated incidents. More often than not they come at the end of a chain – sometimes a very long chain – of tiny happenings. It would stand to reason then, that it is best to read the signs as soon as they occur, in order to save time. This is why divinatory methods can be so useful, as we soon found out. Once we had decided to move to Scotland, everything fell into place with remarkable speed. The right people turned up just at the right time and helped us find our present home, which was the first one we looked at. Shortly after viewing it we consulted the *I Ching (see Chapter 9)* to reassure ourselves that to make an offer right away would be safe. The answer was 'Mission Accomplished'. The wording was so appropriate and encouraging that we went ahead with complete confidence. We owned the house within three days.

I have found again and again that when we are on the right path, when what we are doing is what we are *meant* to be doing, doors open, opportunities present themselves and progress becomes relatively easy. Shortly after moving to Scotland the BBC telephoned me out of the blue and asked to interview me about my work. The programme generated almost 100 calls to the station and as a result my career took off in Scotland. Then a couple of newspapers asked for regular daily and weekly columns. There were many more signs and big and small nudges from the universe. When we first arrived in Glasgow to house-hunt, I kept finding coins on the ground. Not one day passed in that crucial exploratory week when I did not find a few in the street. Although someone once said to me, 'Never stoop for a copper,' I kept picking them up and calling them my 'pennies from heaven'.

If one could learn to read the signs of synchronicity and recognize its promise, fewer 'mistakes' would dog one's life. It is my personal experience that when one becomes aware of synchronicities, they begin to happen more often. Put another way, the more you practise, the luckier you get. When you ask for help from the cosmos it will only be a matter of time before a sign appears. When you need support to take the next step on your journey through life, that support will come. It is my hope that this book will help you to learn to recognize synchronicity in your own life and benefit from it.

WHAT IS SYNCHRONICITY?

CHAPTER ONE

Everything divided and different belongs to one and the same world...

C. G. Jung

The word 'synchronicity' was invented by the Swiss psychologist C. G. Jung in 1929. He first used it publicly in May 1930 in a memorial address for Richard Wilhelm, whose life's work had been the monumental task of translating into German the Chinese 'Book of Changes', the *I Ching*.[1] Apart from a few physicists no one had bothered much about synchronicity until then, although the phenomenon had caught the interest and imagination of German philosophers of the eighteenth and nineteenth centuries. But Jung brought the idea of meaningful coincidences to public attention.

A synchronistic event not only has something uncanny about it, something otherworldly, inexplicable and wondrous, but it also has an important meaning for the person involved. For example, the writer Bill Bryson recounts in *Notes from a Small Island*[2] how he once wanted to write an article about remarkable coincidences and approached a magazine publisher. His proposal was accepted, but he then realized that he did not have enough personal experiences to draw on to make the article interesting enough and wrote to the publishers informing them that he had changed his mind. He left the letter on top of his typewriter and went to work as usual. That very day there happened to be a sale of unwanted books at his office building. When he arrived at the sale, his eyes fell immediately on a book entitled *Remarkable True Coincidences*. A quick glance showed that it contained all the information he needed for his research, but moreover the first example of synchronicity was about a man named Bryson! Most people would believe that all this was just another coincidence, a chance happening without any great significance. But it *was* a significant event, because it brought the writer exactly the information he needed as quickly as possible. Maybe the fact that 'something' made Bryson delay posting his letter and then go to that book sale and find the very book he needed meant that synchronicity itself wanted to be written about...

Bryson's need for information about remarkable coincidences did not *cause* this book to turn up in the book sale. These two things happened at the same time but were, as far as we know, totally independent of one another and the only thing that connected them at all was *meaning*. That is why Jung called synchronicity an 'acausal connecting principle', as opposed to causality, where one thing leads to another or happens *because of* another. Synchronistic movements are not linear, but follow a meandering path and happen spontaneously without planning or warning.

Some people have tried to find rational explanations for synchronistic phenomena, suggesting that perhaps they are a form of telepathy or thought transference. Could it be that at some level everything in this world is connected to everything else, as if we are living in some giant universal mind? Or do we have some kind of antennae that can pick up vital clues and information in situations of great urgency?

Jung warned that it would be hard for many people to accept acausality, to understand that there are situations that no person or thing caused to happen, but that emerged as if from nowhere at just the right time. Aniela Jaffé, one of Jung's most important collaborators, speaks of a 'magical causality', meaning that a link between two apparently unconnected synchronistic events does exist but that it belongs to the realm of magic, being controlled by an intelligence of another dimension.[3] Perhaps the fact that all synchronistic events are preceded by a thought or an idea or a plan of some kind, even if we are only aware of this with hindsight, is an indication that a magical link of some kind does exist.

Marie-Louise von Franz, Jung's closest colleague, who was fascinated by synchronistic phenomena, was worried that no one would be interested in carrying out further investigations.

She even put out an appeal in her book *Psyche and Matter*[4] for her work on this to continue. But synchronicity is elusive. It cannot be ordered or repeated and therefore does not lend itself readily to scientific investigation. It is a bit like trying to prove scientifically that there are such things as dreams. We cannot photograph a dream as proof of its existence. All we have is the empirical evidence.

Furthermore, we can only speak of a synchronistic event when it can be verified by observation. Therefore, synchronicity demands a witness. One of the two events has to be an inner state of being, a psychological attitude or disposition or an intention or a wish, and the other must be an outer *observable* event which mirrors the inner happening.

We have been well trained and socially conditioned to trust only what we can experience with our five outer senses. Yet genuine synchronistic events can only be registered when our normal everyday consciousness is off-guard and their meaning can only be understood if we allow ourselves to 'think' with that other mind of ours, that mind which can make connections that are not obvious at first glance. The trick is to learn to use that other mind with a free spirit and an open heart.

The most interesting aspect of all truly synchronistic phenomena is that there appears to be a pre-existing knowledge of things to come, things of which we have at that moment no apparent awareness whatsoever. There seems to be an altogether 'other' that knows more than us, can see into the future and also has the ingenious ability to find the quickest route to return us to our destined path.

In spite of the absence of 'scientific' evidence that we have a sixth sense, the increase in synchronistic occurrences and the seriousness with which they are now being treated by investigators of paranormal phenomena are indications that the time is probably not far off when we will need to acknowledge the fact that there are dimensions to our minds that are infinitely wiser than our 'normal' consciousness. Jung, Freud and others have done much to draw this to our attention. The conscious mind could be regarded as the tip of the iceberg, with the rest being submerged in the waters of the unconscious. From time to time something of this submerged part breaks through the surface – perhaps in a dream, or as a fantasy or inspiration – and we receive some important information that inspires or gives comfort or is an answer to a prayer. In that moment we are aware that we are not alone, that there is a whole other world 'out there' of which we normally know nothing but which nevertheless reveals itself to us in order to help or warn.

Jung calls this world the 'collective unconscious' and its contents 'archetypes', which in this sense are ordering principles that underlie normal consciousness. Seen from another perspective, they are root images of human experiences – encoded experiences that we all share. There are archetypes of the Mother, Father, God, Self, Fool, Devil, Child, Love, Hate, etc. It is from this realm of archetypal forces, Jung claimed, that we are guided, as if by magic, in certain directions which constitute our individual way through life, the 'individuation process' as he called it. All the archetypes are connected with powerful emotions and ideas and all of them could influence us at any time. *How* we experience them depends on us. The archetypes cannot be known directly in their actual form – just as we cannot *know* electricity, only see and feel its effects. Therefore, they take on guises that we can recognize and that will show us what we need to know.

We understand so little about how, why and by what means other worlds interact with ours that it is probably not accurate even to assume that synchronistic events are acausal, in the sense of 'by no physical cause'. The fact is that we simply don't know. The worlds that lie beyond ours remain mysterious.

The most serious research into these dimensions is taking place in the field of quantum physics. Jung, who collaborated with the Nobel Prize-winning physicist Professor Pauli,[5] was one of the first serious researchers to state that everything, every being and every experience, belongs to the same world. But this one world is not only the world of our known five senses, but a much vaster one which is not perceived in the ordinary way. Therefore, in order for us to get close to, and partake of, some of the benefits of this other reality we need to cultivate a sensitivity and receptivity to its manifestations.

There are various ways in which we can prepare ourselves for what the other side has to offer. We can begin by imagining that 'cracks' between the two worlds appear with great regularity, affording us a glimpse of the altogether 'other' or allowing it to break through into our normally rational, limited and closed minds. If we can start to at least play with the idea that there is more to life than we know or can scientifically prove, then we have taken a big step towards living a more abundant life. There are already telling signs, such as UFO sightings or encounters with angels or astral travelling, that we are becoming increasingly sensitive to wider realities.

Some people need to be persuaded of this intellectually, while others are given an experience that changes their perception overnight. I am reminded of an event that happened when I was driving through the French countryside with my husband early one Sunday morning. As the roads were still empty and driving conditions excellent, I was going a bit faster than I normally would. When we approached a sleepy little village I hardly slowed down. Besides, didn't I have priority as I was on the 'main' road? Well, not in France and not in this village! As we came to the narrow cross-roads in the centre, a large green car pulled into our path from the right. We had no chance of avoiding it; there was no time to stop. All I could do was to shut my eyes and wait for the crash. But when I opened them again we found ourselves on the top of the hill with the village beneath us. I stopped the car and pulled over, unable to speak. We sat there for a long time in absolute shock. We will never know how we escaped a probably fatal accident and how we were transported to safety in a split second. Someone or something had intervened in our fate. But who or what? Could it have been an angel? To us this was undisputed proof that someone was looking out for us, someone or something in possession of unimaginable powers. Later, when we pondered over how and why we were saved, we thought that perhaps it might have been because we were on a pilgrimage. At the time we were writing a travel guide to all the sites in Europe connected with the Holy Grail and the Precious Blood,[6] many of which have themselves witnessed extraordinary synchronistic miracles.

When synchronicity first became a popular subject through the writings of Jung, von Franz and Jaffé, it was considered only to occur at such moments of crisis – including deaths, accidents or passionate love affairs. But it also manifests in apparently unimportant situations. Only a couple of days ago I saw some beautiful Stargazer lilies outside a local shop and went in to buy some. But when I saw the long line of people queueing to pay, I gave up. Half an hour after I arrived back home, my husband came through the door and handed me a bunch of Stargazer lilies! There was no particular reason for this and no great significance revealed itself at a later stage either. Of course, though, when one is writing about synchronicity one can expect synchronistic events to multiply, just to confirm that these things *really do happen*.

I have often wondered why our dream-mind, for instance, will foretell little unimportant events that will happen during the following day, the type of event that seems to have no special meaning. Once I dreamed that a colleague who was due to visit me the next day had changed the colour of her hair. This was precisely what she had done. I take the view that we are being made aware through these little signs that the Otherworld exists and that it is possible to tap into it.

Some people are able to have contact with this Otherworld quite naturally, as if it is second nature to them, while others may need to develop techniques and methods. In either case, to understand its meaning, it is vital that the position of the observer is not altogether lost, that one is *in* the experience but also *observes* it at the same time. Contacting the Otherworld also serves consciousness; each step in this direction could further the development of greater awareness of what it means to be human – and *what else* it might mean to be human.

If we believe that both the conscious *and* the unconscious worlds are but one, ordered by the same divine intelligence, that they are expressions of the same energy, *Unus Mundus* as Jung called it, then we have every reason to train ourselves to become more sensitive to synchronistic revelations and promptings. The most important aspect of synchronicity is the fact that it makes visible to us something of the collective unconscious, or of 'the mind at large', as Aldous Huxley called it, or of some higher intelligence at work.

We need a rainbow bridge between inner and outer realities. Many people all over the world are already building one by means of meditation, dream analysis, active imagination and Rebirthing therapy, to mention but a few ways. We can walk this bridge with our intuition and our feelings, with love and understanding, and leave behind the rules of a scientific worldview as we cross. This needs practice and perseverance and perhaps also a guide who has already crossed that bridge.

In all synchronistic events one is in touch with both worlds; psyche and matter are as one. It is of no importance whether it is our soul or our rational mind that guides us, because in that moment there is no difference.

NOTES

1 Richard Wilhelm, *The I Ching*, Routledge & Kegan Paul, 1951; *see also Chapter 9.*

2 Bill Bryson, *Notes from a Small Island*, Doubleday, 1999.

3 Aniela Jaffé, *The Myth of Meaning*, G. P. Putnam's Sons, 1971.

4 Marie-Louise von Franz, *Psyche and Matter*, Shambhala, 1992.

5 Their work is described in Jung's book *Synchronicity: An Acausal Connecting Principle*, Routledge & Kegan Paul, 1955.

6 Ean and Deike Begg, *In Search of the Holy Grail and the Precious Blood*, Thorsons, 1995.

THE ZIG-ZAG PATH

CHAPTER TWO

Caminante, no hay camino,

Se hace el camino al andar.

Traveller, there is no path,

You make the path as you travel it.

FROM A SONG BY JOAN MANUEL SERRAT

The Warrior is a man who has learned to love life and all the many richnesses it brings him – most of all the path where he walks. There is for the Warrior no greater joy than to walk a path with a heart. On this path he walks, thrilled by the wonder of it all, and in his joy he gives thanks in his heart for this marvellous privilege by embracing everything he encounters with love and gratitude.

THEUN MARES

When you are involved with researching travel guides, as my husband and I are, you quickly realize that when looking for obscure sacred sites or trying to find someone to unlock a remote chapel in a mountain-top graveyard, you cannot rely on ordinary planning. You could not write to a local priest in Spain's Sierra de la Demanda, for instance, and say that you will be there on such and such a day, would they please be available to show you around. You learn soon enough that you need to rely on serendipity and synchronicity to point you in the right direction.

Again and again on our travels we have only been able to gain access to a certain church, museum or private house because we happened to be in the right place at the right time. This does not mean that our path has been smooth! True synchronistic events are always a surprise; they are amazing, sometimes miraculous and frequently amusing, but at times also frightening. The path often leads in the opposite direction and then you end up in the 'wrong' place, but find out later that it was exactly where you needed to be. At the time, though, you might curse yourself for having made such a foolish 'mistake', wondering what on Earth you are doing there when you 'should' or would rather be somewhere else.

This is what happened to us on one of our trips to Ireland. We were researching sites connected with the Celtic magician Merlin and were driving through remote countryside when we noticed a warning light flashing on the control panel. We stopped the car and searched the manual for information about what to do. 'Do not stop the engine,' the book warned, 'and drive straight to the nearest garage.' Well, can you imagine reading that in the middle of nowhere, far from any town that might have a garage? Worse still, many of the roads looked the same and had no signposts. We took in a couple more sites, but left the motor running. We made a wish at a prayer-tree and then headed for the town of Waterford, in the south of the Irish Republic, and hoped for the best. We found a garage that could deal with our make of car, but it was shut for lunch for the next two hours. We turned off the engine and waited in blazing heat until a mechanic returned. We told him about the warning light and he went straight to the problem. He pulled out a small wire, put it back in again, asked me to start the engine and hey presto, the car started perfectly. 'Nothing wrong,' he assured us. 'Probably just a bit of dust that set off the warning light.'

This all seemed a bit bizarre to us. Why should the car behave in such a way? We continued our journey and after approximately 20 miles I started to browse through the index of our *Irish AA Roadbook* – a habit I had got into – in order to find place-names which might suggest a connection with ancient mysteries. What I found was the mention of a Merlin's Cave a mere few minutes' taxi ride from Waterford. All that time we had waited by the garage we could so easily have gone to the cave and photographed it and there would still have been time to have spoken to someone in the local bar about the history of the place. But, alas, we had missed an important synchronistic nudge. Again and again such things happened, but we were often too slow to pick up on them. It is only with hindsight that we realized that divine guidance was at hand all the time.

On another occasion, this time on a trip to Germany when we were writing about Holy Grail places, we discovered that we had left the computer lead for my laptop in London. This was annoying as we wanted to write up each day's visit that same night. We were unable to replace the lead in Hamburg, our first port of call, but were given the address of a firm in Brunswick which might be able to help. Brunswick is the traditional home of Till Eulenspiegel, Germany's fourteenth-century arch-trickster, who was famous for his mischievous antics. But the tricks he was to play on us were entirely beneficent and saved us a great deal of time – in the end. Having no intention of making the tiresome detour to Brunswick, we decided to do without the lead and drive to Magdeburg, as planned. But the 'trickster' had other plans. The motorway exit we needed was closed. Rather reluctantly we decided to drop in on the computer firm after all. But we knew that the museums we were interested in would be shut as it was a Monday. That was why we had planned to go to Brunswick at a later date. As it happens, one of the museums there is the home of the Onyx Vessel, a priceless relic believed to have come from the Temple of Solomon in Jerusalem.

It took us a long time to find the computer firm and the man we needed was out to lunch. When he got back it was to inform us that we had come in vain, they did not have our make of lead in stock. Rather fed up, we decided to go for a bite to eat at the station, opposite the tourist office. Whilst we were waiting for our food to arrive, I popped across to the tourist office 'just in case'. Without hesitation, they gave me a telephone number to ring. After many phone calls I finally reached the museum's curator at home, whilst he was having his lunch. When he heard that we were writing a book about the Grail and that we had information on an obscure precious cup from Mantua in Italy, he invited us to meet him at the museum straight away and said that he personally would show us the Vessel, which was housed in a part of the museum that was off-limits to the public and would not be on view again until the following year. Doctor Walz turned out to be the most patient and charming of guides; not only did he allow us to take photographs of the Vessel from all angles, but he also had photocopies made of important and rare documents relating to the fascinating history of the vase.

I have given this account at length because it is important to see how at almost every turn there is an overshadowing presence that has a will of its own and that will find a way to ensure that we follow the easiest route to achieve our goal. Sometimes one feels a fool at getting lost, but I have long given up getting upset when I go down a wrong road or, indeed, turn up at the wrong airport.

One of the most amusing zig-zag paths we took was in Brittany, in France, near a small town called Trehorenteuc. We were after a photograph of the mysterious and enchanting lake in the Val-sans-Retour (Valley of No Return). We had parked in the car park on the edge of a forest and saw a sign leading up a path to the valley. After half an hour we had not seen another sign and we were still *climbing*. We had left my 12-year-old son at the hotel and I was anxious about the time. After another hour there was no sign of the lake and we were still only walking *around* the forest. We decided to listen for water and turned into lush woods. Eventually we could hear running water and after a short while came upon a thin stream. It began to rain and was getting dark. We had no idea how long this exploration would still take and then we had to walk all the way back again! But we ploughed on. When you do research you become obsessive and everything else has to take second place, although I was worried about leaving my son for so long. Finally we began to run, as it was getting increasingly dark, and then the most luminous lake appeared before us, hidden and protected by the forbidding forest, just as it was described in the legend of Morgan-le-Fay and Lancelot. Enough light was still entering from the sky above the lake for me to take a series of photographs.

We were about to retrace our path through the woods when we saw three hikers with heavy backpacks come out of the trees on the other side of the water. Without thinking about it, I walked round and asked them whether they knew a quick way back to the car park. 'Just through those trees,' they pointed back in the direction they had come. We walked down a little path for less than a minute, and there was the car park and the town beyond it. We had come full circle. For us it really had turned out to be the Valley of No Return, a valley in which one gets lost – loses oneself in order to find oneself. Without getting lost we would not have had the full experience of the valley. And then, just as we had come to the end of our journey and were about to go all the way back again, no doubt in pitch darkness for most of the way, there was the synchronistic meeting with the hikers. On our return to the hotel we found my son happily lying on his bed reading a book.

How often we lost our way only to find that serendipity had led us straight down the zig-zag path to where we needed to go. Sometimes we found things that we were not even seeking, but that were significant nevertheless, as happened on one occasion in Spain. As always around lunch-time, the search began for the best picnic site, preferably one beside a cool stream. We would gladly drive a mile or two out of our way in order to have shade and water. But this time we had been driving for longer than usual and were about to settle for a stop by the roadside when my intuition led me on just a little further. And then we did find a perfect site, with shade and a lake for a swim.

Afterwards we continued along this road, rather than go back the way we had come, hoping that it might be a shortcut to the main road. We passed a little church and stopped to look inside. It was shut, of course – this was Spain on a hot afternoon. But as we made our way back to the car, the priest came running after us to see if there was anything he could do for us. We told him that we were researching Black Virgin sites and just wondered whether there was one in his church. He smiled, said, 'Come,' and took us back inside where there was a magnificent statue of a Black Madonna and Child. 'This is Our Lady of Casbas,' the priest said proudly. And before we left he gave us a huge colour poster of Her.

When we learn to follow our nose, life takes on a friendlier appearance. When normal consciousness is dimmed so that we become aware of signals from the Otherworld, we become witness to a totally different world, which none the less is part of this one. What constitutes the boundary between these two worlds remains a mystery, but we know that it can be penetrated by human consciousness, and perhaps also physically. The signs may be confusing and hard to decipher, but if we follow them we may just get there in the end.

Often when we were walking in forests or deserted countryside, looking for a particular tree or standing stone, we had only our intuition to rely on. We might see a stick pointing in a particular direction and follow it, or there might be a paint-mark on a tree, not a signpost really, but we would take it as such anyway. Once a sparrow-hawk flew ahead of us in the Forest of Brocéliande, in France, and showed us the way to a sacred well. It is my belief that when one is on the trail of sacred sites, one gets closer to nature and begins to read nature's otherworldly signs.

When one is on such a journey, there is just one thing to do and that is not to plan ahead too rigidly. You invariably end up somewhere else, in a different country even, but that is where you are meant to be. This happened to us when we were researching place-names that were mentioned in Wolfram von Eschenbach's early thirteenth-century epic poem *Parzival*. We were in Austria, looking for Pettau, the birthplace of the Grail-Knight's grandfather, and had been asking tourist offices and cultural attachés in vain for some time. We had all but given up, assuming that in most likelihood it was a fictitious name. But then, in Wolfram's own home town, Eschenbach, we discovered that Pettau was now the Slovenian Ptuj. Our car insurance did not cover us to drive in Slovenia, but we risked it anyway. Our long detour was well rewarded. In the tourist office of the little town of Ptuj there was a giant-sized copy of a magnificent map dating from 1678. On it were marked all the strange-sounding names from Wolfram's poem, which proved that they had really existed. Furthermore, it appeared that Parzival himself was potentially an historic character.[1] For a researcher, such finds are priceless and the support of synchronistic phenomena is vital.

The story of the Grail-Knight Perceval is that of a young innocent fool who is learning to become a man by undergoing various initiatory experiences. He travels the zig-zag path, at first unconsciously, making many mistakes, upsetting many people and never asking for advice, but something drives him on. Briefly the story goes like this:

Perceval is brought up alone in a forest by his widowed mother who tries to ensure that he knows nothing of chivalry lest she lose him, like his father and brothers. Nevertheless, when he encounters three knights, whom he takes to be angels, he goes off in search of adventure, at which his mother dies of grief. He reaches the Court of King Arthur, where he avenges the Queen by killing a knight who has insulted her and stolen the royal cup.

In search of further adventures, Perceval arrives at the court of the Fisher King, who gives him a sword. He witnesses a procession in which a squire carries a white lance, from the point of which a drop of blood runs down on to his hand. Among other marvels there follows a

beautiful damsel holding a Grail which emits a brilliant light. A magnificent banquet is served during which the Grail again passes before Perceval, but he does not ask the important question, which is: 'Whom does the Grail serve?' – in other words, 'What is going on here?'

The next morning there is no one around and all the splendour has disappeared. Then Perceval meets a damsel mourning her dead lover. She reveals to him that the Fisher King has been wounded in the thigh and that he would have been healed if Perceval had asked about the spear and the Grail. Unless this happens the King cannot die and hand over the guardianship of the Grail to a new king.

Perceval tries to find the way back to the Grail castle in vain. After many years of wandering he finally admits defeat, drops the reins of his horse and says, 'I have looked everywhere possible. I cannot go on. Go, horse, take me where you will. I accept whichever place you stop at.'

The horse takes him to a hermit who lives in a cave and he reveals to Perceval his true identity, which is the appointed heir to the Grail, and thus helps him to remember himself. Perceval then becomes the next Grail-King.

Perceval's story is also the story of the evolution of the human soul. We all set out as the fool who needs to learn the ways of the world. Our quest is to find the Holy Grail, that place in which our soul has its home. Like Perceval we may make some terrible mistakes. It is only when Perceval turns *away* from his goal and gives up the ways of the world and lets his horse (his instincts) guide him that he is led to the wise teacher, the one who has always known who he is and what his purpose is. Likewise, if we follow our instincts, drop the reins and let destiny guide us, we will get there, although the road leads first here, then there, up hill and down dale. When we are on a mountain top we can survey the whole terrain and feel on top of the world, but then we come down again, no longer see the big picture and are lost once more. And so the journey continues. All we can do is put one foot in front of the other and have the courage to follow the small voice within, observe the subtle signposts and, above all, trust that there is divine guidance and that all our sufferings and all our joys are part of the journey.

NOTES

1 For a full account of the story of Parzival *see* Ean and Deike Begg, *In Search of the Holy Grail and the Precious Blood*, Thorsons, 1995.

FLIRTING

CHAPTER THREE

As far as you can, be a slave, not a monarch.

Let yourself be struck. Be the ball and not the bat.

RUMI

We had just arrived in Majorca for a holiday with our friends Sarah and Richard and were on our way to St Elmo in the far south-west of the island. It was extremely hot by 11 in the morning and we stopped for a refreshing beer at a roadside bar with seats outside. Our friends had just been to an Arnold Mindell[1] workshop, where he had introduced them to the idea of the universe flirting with people. As they were telling us about it, a sudden gust of wind dislodged a piece of cellophane from the gutter and carried it a few feet into the air. Then it landed on the road again and ran, jumped and flew in little tight circles before it was lifted up high again. This little dance with the wind went on for a considerable while and at times it looked as if it were performing especially for us. We were laughing till tears ran down our cheeks. 'This,' proclaimed Richard, 'is what is meant by the universe flirting with us!'

'To flirt' in its original sense means 'to give a light blow' and 'to jerk away'. How apt this is for synchronicities that give us a light blow – sometimes not so light – and a jerk.

All through that holiday we were aware of shooting stars, jumping fish, unusual cloud formations and the strange behaviour of birds. The most remarkable synchronicity occurred one afternoon after my husband had been reading Sir Laurens van der Post's account of how Jung had announced his death to him by means of a seagull while he was on a liner headed for South Africa.[2] Van der Post himself had died shortly before our holiday and in his last letter to my husband he had said, 'We shall meet before long.' While my husband was dozing he became aware of a praying mantis crawling across the fly-screen of the window, its triangular face peering at him. None of us had ever seen a mantis in Majorca before. The next passage that Ean read in the book alluded to the Kalahari Bushmen, of whom van der Post had been a great and knowledgeable friend, and whose totem animal, the praying mantis, he shared. After his sleep, my husband continued to read and in the next paragraph found the only reference to a mantis in the book. Van der Post always kept his word and with supreme courtesy was clearly saying his farewell.

I was reminded of this new twist on flirting once more when I recently read a review of the Oscar-winning film

American Beauty. Director Sam Mendes had once observed a dance of the wind and a plastic bag much like our piece of cellophane. He was so struck by what he perceived as an overwhelming beauty that he recreated the scene for the film and made a major feature of it.

I once had a tree flirt with me. We were looking after a friend's cat on a remote farm in Majorca one summer. Each day we drove out to feed the cat and had a picnic in the orchard. Late one hot afternoon, after we had packed up to go home, for no reason at all I wanted to put my spine against one of the larger trees. As I was leaning against the age-old trunk I felt the sudden and strong desire for chocolate. My husband said that we could stop in the village and buy some. 'No, not that kind of chocolate, I want the dark real stuff,' I replied quite firmly. Then I looked up and realized that I was standing beneath a carob tree, from which an alternative chocolate is produced! I am not a lover of chocolate, which made this event all the more remarkable. Within minutes the desire had subsided, but I felt deliciously refreshed just the same.

Not only can the natural world flirt with us, but so can our own bodies, through body language. They also give strong signals indicating when there is a powerful reaction to an outer trigger which has not yet been registered by the conscious mind. Tamara, a young woman, had been quite relaxed until I asked her whether she had any major fears. She shook her head and shrugged her shoulders. But when I said, 'You know, like fear of spiders or fear of birds,' she suddenly closed up by crossing her arms and legs, and then proceeded to tell me in a shaky voice about an incident in childhood when she was locked into a chicken house for several hours as punishment for throwing stones. It was this fear that she really needed to talk about, because from that day on she had re-experienced the original trauma whenever she came across a bird in a confined space. Each time a bird flew into her house, she would shut the door on the room it was in and had to wait until someone came to catch and release it. This had at times made life extremely awkward.

Our feelings and bodies also help us to understand hidden meanings by making songs synchronistically pop into our heads at crucial moments. This happened to my friend Mary. She had announced to her husband that she had arranged to meet a friend with whom she had fallen out. Now Mary, who dislikes any kind of conflict, felt guilty and wanted to kiss and make up, and had arranged to meet her friend in a bar. But when she told her husband, he started humming 'It's the wrong time and the wrong place'. Mary asked him why that tune. 'I suppose I don't think that it is the right time to meet just yet,' was his answer. He was quite right, because, as it happened, the friend cancelled the meeting, still angry.

We need to listen to and respect these little promptings from the psyche. Even if we can't do anything about them, at least they can serve as a warning or an affirmation or an encouragement. My daughter once brought a new boyfriend to a party I was giving for a special birthday. When she introduced us she said, 'This is Joe,' and I took his outstretched hand and said, 'Goodbye!' I did not recall this afterwards and if it hadn't been for various witnesses I would not have believed it. In the event that boyfriend turned out to be a lot of trouble. My unconscious mind had obviously known from the start, even though on the conscious level I thought him quite a nice chap, and the 'other in me' had taken the opportunity to show me that something wasn't right.

If we are aware of the Other, we are more likely to encounter synchronistic events. One way to do this is to spend time on your own. These times need to be quiet and tranquil. It does not matter what you do as long as you are silent. You could scrub the floor, meditate, do yoga or sort out old papers. I learned this quite involuntarily when I was 20 and spent a year in Brussels in a large, almost empty apartment. I was alone much of the time and after a while I started talking to myself out loud and began to feel that I was in conversation with someone else. I also played mind games with myself and learned to remember more than 100 words in sequence by making up stories out of random words. I started buying books on psychology; it was as if the invisible one had encouraged me to. It was in Brussels that I started reading about subjects like inner development and visualization.

Silence gives intuition a chance to perceive what our ordinary senses cannot, to 'see' images and ideas which arise from the unconscious just when they are needed. Every artist knows this. It is in the silent moments that we literally hear our thoughts and the songs that bring the message. When the unconscious mind hits the right note we receive a light blow and jerk away. We are amazed. 'Eureka!' we exclaim. And then we must do something about it, honour the other's gift. Sometimes the blow is not so light and we are, figuratively speaking, blown away.

It is through silence that we give Fate a chance to flirt with us. Once, in Barbados, it was that silent creature, the crab, that flirted with me and led me towards hidden treasure. I love this story because it is one in which justice can be seen to be done. My husband was taking part in an inspection tour of the hotels of the island and I went along for the fun and perhaps also to do some astrological chart readings during the times when he would be busy. Someone must have gone to the police and told them that I was engaged in 'illegal trading', because on the third morning three police officers turned up at our hotel and arrested me. I was due to join the others for lunch in two hours and had no way of getting in touch. The police kept me waiting in a very hot room for a very long time. Eventually they were persuaded that I was just an innocent tourist and I joined the party just in time for dessert.

Afterwards I went body surfing in the warm blue sea with its spectacular waves. Out of the corner of my eye I noticed a rather large crab disappearing under some rocks. I got out of the water to follow it. Peering under the rocks I saw a most enormous shell, its mother of pearl glistening, beckoning me to come and get it. It was too far away for me to reach it from where I was. I had to climb up over the top and then down into the rocky chaos. On my way down I found a wallet, wedged between two small rocks, containing a few hundred dollars. It looked as though it had been lying there for years. It was full of sand and there was no name in it. Back at the hotel I laundered the money and hung it up to dry. It was roughly the amount I might have earned had I done a few chart readings.

We had a suspicion who the taleteller was, as only one other person, apart from the inspection team, knew that I was on the island. The following day news came that this person's house had been invaded by a green monkey that not only made an awful mess on her terrace but also tore up a valuable antique Chinese screen.

If we are on good terms with the Other, we don't need to make a huge effort in order to read the signs, such as the crab and shell which caught my attention. During quiet times we have a chance to open to deeper layers of our psyche. When the body is thus occupied the higher or deeper mind can kick in.

Conscious thinking can be a great obstacle to the messages from the other side. Madame Blavatsky writes that the mind is the greatest slayer of the truth.[3] In other words, ordinary consciousness is limited in what it can perceive and understand and therefore assumes a subjective standpoint. Truth is always far greater than we could possibly grasp. Our personal truth will always be conditioned by who we are and by our personal experiences. But when we gain access to the Otherworld we catch a glimpse of another reality altogether, one that does not lend itself to analysis and rationalization. In this other world our set of rules no longer applies.

I once encountered a situation where my body became the instrument of intuition and told me in no uncertain terms that something of the greatest importance was happening. It was shortly before my twenty-eighth birthday and it completely changed the course of my life. That one synchronistic experience is continuing to influence all I do. It set up a completely new chain of causes and effects and put my whole existence onto a path I would never consciously have chosen.

I was driving past a bookshop with a large notice on its window saying 'Closing Down Sale'. Well, that sign was surely flirting with me and I stopped to have a look. There, right in the middle of the display, I saw *The Complete Astrologer*.[4] In that instant I felt is if I had been struck by lightning. I went into a kind of shock and after what seemed an awfully long time, started tingling all over. I began to worry, as I couldn't understand what was happening to me. I just stood and stared. It is quite unbelievable, but although I had always had a vague interest in astrology, I didn't actually know that there were books about it. My mother used to read out our astrological forecasts from the newspapers and occasionally would talk to us about our individual zodiacal characteristics, but it was all just a bit of fun. Now, here in front of me, was the most amazing sight: a large book on astrology! Of course I had to buy it, as a present to myself for my birthday.

That night I sat up and read and read. By 2 a.m. I had drawn up my own chart. It was the most extraordinary experience, apart from giving birth, I had ever had. Now I had the problem of verifying my calculations. I was far too excited to go to sleep. I had never known what I wanted to do with my life and now suddenly I knew in an instant, without registering the full significance of it, that I had found my vocation. I wrote a letter to Derek and Julia Parker, the authors of the book, asking for information about how to learn more about astrology. A few days later I received a reply from Julia. Not only did she explain how to check the calculations, but she also gave me information about the Faculty of Astrological Studies, whose President she was at the time, and included a leaflet about the Astrological Association of Great Britain.

I wanted to start studying with the Faculty straight away, but had no money. I had just found this amazing treasure, but had no means of taking it further. But I was determined to somehow make my dream come true and had an idea. I put an advert in a local shop window advertising my services as a curtain maker. I was not trained in sewing, but somehow had taught myself to make curtains. The very next day a person came who had just bought a three-storey house and wanted curtains for all the windows.

This was synchronicity number one. Synchronicity number two was that she turned out to be the new owner of the bookshop where I had made my precious purchase. She kept me working for long enough to pay for my first astrology course and all the books I needed, plus an electric sewing machine to replace my antique hand-operated one. It all happened very fast from then on. I quickly progressed in my studies and within a year I was on the council of the Astrological Association, running their London meetings.

I know for certain that had I not had such a strong bodily reaction that I would not have bought that book. As I had no money, books were not a priority. But the signals had been impossible for me to ignore. Astrology had flirted with me and I had fallen in love with it. What's more, it rewarded me richly. And although I subsequently trained as a psychotherapist and Rebirther, astrology has remained my first love. Now, 28 years later, I have started a new cycle, with astrology once more becoming the main player in my life and my main source of income.

My philosophy, which was a gift from my maternal grandfather, has always been 'You never know what's round the corner.' I take the optimistic view. Shawn, a young lawyer, on the other hand, always expects the worst – 'You never know what's round the corner and it could be a nightmare' – because he is frightened of being disappointed. He cannot bring himself to understand that expecting the worst can actually help to attract it. In all cases of attitude problems the first step is to develop a policy of positive expectation. Negative thoughts create negative thought-forms, which in turn attract negative events, whilst positive thoughts create positive thought-forms and attract positive events, i.e. energy follows thought. Even if nothing good happens immediately, at least with a positive attitude you will feel better in the meantime. A positive attitude towards life entails taking responsibility for *all* our actions and experiences. It means that we can no longer apportion blame or guilt to anyone or anything; we need to look closely at ourselves and the part we have always played in the great drama that is our existence.

No matter how negative our response to life's offerings, however, the flirting will continue. Each day brings new opportunities. Destiny calls again and again, and our path is strewn with little reminders of who we are and in which direction we need to go next. It may take time to decipher the message, years even, but if we are alert to what life brings each day, we have a chance to hear the call sooner rather than later.

Habitual emotional reactions will prevent us from noticing synchronicities. If, on the other hand, our responses become more spontaneous, synchronicities will magically increase and pull us this way and that, act as warnings and confirmations, open and close doors accordingly.

I remember in every detail the day I received my first English reading book, at the age of 10, at school in Hamburg. On the front page was an aerial photograph of London's Trafalgar Square with its four lions and red double-decker buses, and there, in the middle, stood Nelson on his column. I felt a tremendous thrill. I had never seen the picture before, yet I *knew* this place. I kept looking and looking at it. The pages were still stiff and I opened the book, buried my face in it and kissed the pages. Although I had no conscious plans then to live in England, and never gave it any further thought, by the age of 17 I had moved to London.

The path that is uniquely ours is our own responsibility to find and to follow. We cannot blame our parents, partners, society or God for preventing us from treading it. Unless we stop blaming we have no chance at all to begin living our own precious lives. Blaming means giving away our power. We are in effect saying that other people have power over us to hold us back and make us miserable. As a psychotherapist and astrologer I see people who have had the most appalling lives of abuse and hardship. Yet they have pulled through and have become philosophical, and quite often come to view their awesome experiences as a necessary learning curve – a first-hand course in psychology so to speak.

When we realize that we can take our lives into our own hands, that we have great power, that our lives have purpose and that our task is to fulfil that purpose, we begin to stretch ourselves, mentally, emotionally and spiritually. We can then be outrageous in the sense that we can begin to go to the limits of our abilities. This may shock others and even ourselves at first, but what you might regard as outrageous today will become, in the Buddhist sense, 'everyday thing' tomorrow. To be outrageous in this sense is to do what excites you, even the apparently impossible. You could change your life right now by doing something shocking, something that goes against the grain and against accepted convention, but that at the same time brings forth a part of unlived life from within you.

A married woman in her early thirties, whose marriage was in difficulty, consulted me about a dilemma she found herself in. She came from a small rural town where every one knew each other. Her husband was the local vet and her family had lived in the area for two generations. She revealed that she had been on anti-depressants for 18 years. She was in a constant daze, couldn't think straight and couldn't hold down a job. She had become convinced, especially by her husband, that she was mentally ill and had to stay on drugs for the rest of her life. Each time she tried to come off them, she could see quickly that her marriage was a farce and started to rebel. But her husband, her doctor and the religious sect she belonged to would put pressure on her to resume her medication. Not one person in all those years had bothered to talk to her about her problems or helped her look at her drug dependency. But now she had fallen for a new man and wanted out of her marriage.

In the end she needed little encouragement from me. The love of the other man provided enough incentive to come off the pills and take a good hard look at how her husband had kept her 'asleep' and under his control. She moved out, leaving her children in the marital home, got a job and a divorce, and recovered her health and sanity. In the eyes of her family and community these were outrageous things and she was ostracized. She followed her heart and ultimately her destiny. But in order to do so she had to face the seemingly impossible.

If we take the view that this woman was weak-willed, that she needed to learn to stand on her own two feet, we can see how she was thrown a lifeline in the only way she could understand at that time and would respond to. When destiny flirted with her she winked in response and changed her life.

Many people lead a life that is not right for them. Perhaps it has no purpose, perhaps it is too one-sided, perhaps they simply got stuck on the wrong track. They are quite unconscious of the possibility of a more abundant life and don't recognize it when it is flirting with them.

If the necessary changes are not made, however, the body may give strong signals by becoming sick, or a relationship might fail, or a person might fall into a deep depression. Yet frequently people persist in holding on to entrenched life patterns, waiting without hope. The call is not heard, the flirting not responded to and there is no awareness of promising synchronistic events. Feelings are often totally shut down, and as for intuition, well, that would be far too dangerous to listen to. So people get stuck until there is an emergency, or disaster strikes, which may force the necessary changes.

The secret lies in letting go. But what does that really mean? How can we let go when it's all getting on top of us and we have family responsibilities and a demanding job? Perhaps a disturbing dream will tell us that our soul is in peril, that our health is deteriorating and that we need to slow down. But try telling this to the boss!

In my experience, the first step in letting go is to see the present life situation exactly as it is, neither blaming ourselves nor others but realizing that something has to change. At such times we are in a period of *liminality*, in a no man's land between two major sections of our life. The past has outlived its usefulness but the future has not yet arrived. There are things that need to be done. Something inside has to shift in order to make that decisive new move.

Hexagram 6 of the *I Ching*[5] is called 'Waiting' and is about waiting with the view that all beings have need of nourishment from above 'but the gift of food comes in its own time, and for that one must wait'. Clouds in the sky announce that rain will soon fall and will 'quietly fortify the body with food and drink and the *mind with gladness and good cheer*. Fate comes when it will, and thus we are ready.' Waiting with gladness and good cheer, rather than sadness and no hope, is the attitude which will attract a new synchronicity.

The Tarot card 'The Hanged Man' is also about this period of suspense. It is not a comfortable position to be in. The Hanged Man is suspended by one leg, hanging upside-down and losing his old values, symbolized by coins falling from his pockets, yet he has a benign smile on his face. This card is about the acceptance of a necessary suspension that precedes a new way of thinking. First we need to suspend all expectations and turn our thinking on its head and our values upside-down. This takes place on the threshold between the inner and outer worlds. A period of suspense, of not knowing, is necessary to acquire the knowledge and tools with which to bring about a fundamental and profound shift, a new view of reality.

This waiting phase can be very difficult and many are those who would rather do anything than live through it. Yet, as borne out by psychotherapy, with persistence there comes a point when one can pronounce, 'I could never turn back now.' When that moment arrives we know that we are on our way and the dreams that accompany this transition frequently confirm that a deep process of transformation has begun.

Our very thinking, about anything at all, will create frequency waves, and what we send out to the world returns to us. The smallest attempt to think with positive intent will begin a new chain reaction of events. Even wishing to be shown how to start, how to reach our path, will elicit a flirting response from the universe.

As soon as we are on our way synchronicities come hard and fast and life becomes 'easy' in that we no longer try to *make* something happen but rather *allow* it to happen. This is what letting go really means: making space in our lives for something new to come into being. And with that 'something new' the synchronistic flirting begins all over again.

The *intention* of keeping an eye on our moods is often enough, if remembered daily, to raise our energy frequency and take us to another level of consciousness. That is why flirting and synchronistic events then begin to multiply. You are starting to live your life with the inclusion of your other, *inner*, five senses. These are needed because many synchronistic phenomena cannot be picked up with our ordinary consciousness. The connections are too subtle, in both receiving and sending clues.

People sometimes wonder how they can tell the difference between an intuitive insight and a random hunch. Initially this might be difficult and only time will tell. If an idea, a plan or a coincidence is nothing more than a hunch, it will get weaker with time, but if it comes from intuition, or is confirmed by a synchronistic event, it will get stronger. The fact that we have noted an event is enough to keep us alert to further synchronicities along the way.

Timing is also a factor. As mentioned earlier, sometimes synchronicity tells us something by *desencuentros*, by non-meetings, in order to draw our attention to the fact that the time is not ripe for a certain undertaking. It is vital that we understand this, for not only can we waste a great deal of time going down the wrong track, or round in circles, but we could also do harm to ourselves and others by insisting that where there is a will there is a way.

Individuals who are sensitive to their inner promptings listen to dreams, check their feelings and ask for advice *(see Chapter 9)*. If you are not already in the habit of letting synchronicities guide you, you have not yet discovered the way of least activity, the way of *wu wei*, which is the way of active passivity, the watchfulness of a tiger. When we make the switch from controlling every small aspect of our lives to allowing things to happen, allowing order to arise out of apparent chaos, we change our thinking, and when we change our thinking we change our minds.

Most of us are too impatient to let the other guide us, but when we let the other flirt with us, it will become an active player and true companion.

NOTES

1 Arnold Mindell is the developer of process-oriented-psychology and the author of several books, including *The Dream Body*, Sigo Press, 1982.

2 Laurens van der Post, *Yet Being Someone Other*, Penguin, 1982.

3 Helena P. Blavatsky, *The Secret Doctrine*, The Theosophical Publishing Society, 1888. Helena Blavatsky (1831–1891) founded the Theosophical Society in 1875.

4 Derek and Julia Parker, *The Complete Astrologer*, Mitchell Beazley, 1971.

5 Richard Wilhelm, *The I Ching*, Routledge & Kegan Paul, 1951.

MOTIVATION, INTENTION AND PURPOSE

CHAPTER FOUR

With will, fire becomes sweet water,
and without will, even water becomes fire.

RUMI

In our ordinary existence there is no perception of the Otherworld. We cannot distinguish between this world and the other, between what is within ourselves and what is without. It is only when something extraordinary happens that we sit up with a jerk and wonder what on Earth is going on. The purpose of synchronicity is to give us that jerk, that blow, to remind us of who we may be, and a way to read into the universe at large.

Anything, absolutely anything, will do to get our energy moving. It does not matter what motivates us at the outset of our journey, as long as we can snap out of our spiritual inertia and start moving. If our health has been less than perfect, we may be motivated to regain our energy and as a result we join a fitness centre, get up 30 minutes earlier each morning and work out. As we regain our health and our energy returns we might become more interested in the world around us and as a result might meet new people who will influence the course of our life from now on. If we are poor, we may be motivated to earn money and as a result attend a course in a subject which will lead sooner or later to a qualification that will provide good employment.

'Whatever turns you on', as Fritz Perls taught in Gestalt therapy in the sixties. And whatever our motivation, it will be fuelled by some kind of pain or suffering. We may be discontented in a general sense and wonder whether there is more to life than our present existence or we may be suffering from a specific pain such as the loss of a loved one. But whenever we reach that point where life's meaning seems to elude us, we invariably ask, 'What is the meaning of my life?' The question is already the beginning of the search for the lost self. If we keep on asking an answer will come sooner or later.

When I was 23, I was plunged without warning into what St John of the Cross called 'the dark night of the soul', what Jung referred to as 'the night sea journey'. Life's meaning suddenly totally disappeared. My husband was a performing musician and was on the road for much of the time and I was spending long hours on my own with only my baby daughter to talk to. One stormy night, as I sat by the fire listening to music, the unconscious broke through quite unexpectedly and with a fury. It felt like a huge chasm appearing without warning in front of me, threatening to swallow me up. I was convinced that I was on the very point of going mad, that I could keep my hold on reality no longer. I took a cold shower, hoping for an anti-shock effect, gradually calmed down and the next day all was well again.

Two weeks later the same thing happened, this time in the form of undifferentiated fear. My whole body felt as if it had become invaded by all the horrors of the universe. This time I did not recover so quickly. I stayed in this condition for several weeks, with a racing heartbeat, shallow breathing and total loss of appetite. The doctor prescribed tranquillizers, but I flushed them down the loo and sought the help of a healer instead. The first thing he did was to teach me how to breathe properly and calm myself by practising a slow rhythm. It worked in that I became less anxious, but I could still see no meaning to my existence. Even my daughter, whom I loved dearly, seemed only a responsibility I felt I could no longer carry. People told me to pull myself together. If only I could.

The desire to leave this meaningless life altogether began to grow inside. If it hadn't been for my daughter I would probably have followed that urge. My life force had completely stopped flowing outward. Nothing was any longer of the slightest interest, nothing caught my eye and 'flirted' with me. It was as if my soul had departed.

Those who have similar experiences will know of the agony of waking in the morning without the motivation to get up and wishing that life would go away. You drag yourself through the day from morning to night only to begin again the next day, and the next. When you are on the night sea journey there is no sign of hope or meaning and no conception of purpose.

I was not yet familiar with the phrase 'lose yourself so you can find yourself'. I didn't know then that what I was going through was a process in which the ego (our conscious thinking and controlling self) has to stand aside and watch the psyche being taken apart bit by bit. At the time I had no choice in the matter.

It took several months before I felt anything near approaching 'normal' again. I divorced my husband, left the countryside and moved back to London. Looking back, I could blame my breakdown cum breakthrough on our move to the country and the isolation that followed. But now I can see that the process by which the ego's protective shell is broken down, creating an opening to the Otherworld, a world buzzing with promise and new possibilities, was essential for my individuation process.

One morning I woke up with the realization that 'it' was over. A mental realignment had taken place and my life's work was soon to begin. I began to read with an astonishing fervour for the first time in my life. Because I am dyslexic I have always had to be extremely careful in my choice of reading material, as it always took forever to read a book all the way through. But I was motivated by my newfound passion for life and my reading skills improved dramatically. Five years later I heard the call and began studying astrology. My vocation had begun.

Suddenly my life had meaning again. I was going to be an astrologer, which to me was a miracle. I had never imagined that there was anything special that I could do. I had studied languages and had used them in working for an international music publisher, but that had not brought any satisfaction or meaning at all. Now I had come across something amazing: a way of looking at the universe that made sense. *I was motivated.*

I have found that as soon as one is motivated, in however banal or feeble a way, synchronicity will begin to show the next step, which is never far away. In fact it is right there where we are standing now. It may be a very simple and obvious step but, as Jung tells us, 'Simple things are always the most difficult but if one does the next and most necessary thing without fuss and with conviction, one is always doing something meaningful and intended by fate.'[1]

In my case, I had an awful lot of unfinished business to catch up with, an awful lot of living to do and my vocation would be the way in which I could do that. From now on I became aware of synchronistic events. When I joined the Astrological Association I was amazed to find that its President and Chairman lived just five minutes from the house I had recently moved to. Many other things happened to confirm that I was now on the right road. I was building up a practice in no time at all and frequently met the 'right' person who pointed to the next step.

The German poet Rilke thought that the problem with humanity was that we are too impatient. We are always trying to get somewhere or get out of something. Yet the future arrives when it will and not before. When we finally know that a divine order guides us we will understand that, in the words of Aniela

Jaffé, 'What at the beginning of the way was sheer unconsciousness and emptiness, or appeared commonplace, now contains the secret of simplicity in which the opposites unite.'[2]

INTENTION

I once found myself working in therapy with five men who all expressed the intention of joining a gym. But each one had a different motivation. One, a young man who did not need to work for a living, couldn't see the point of getting up in the morning. He was overweight and lethargic and wanted to join the gym in order to lose a bit of weight and to have something to get up for. Another wanted to get fit and raise his energy levels. A third still saw himself as a 15 year old, tall, thin and awkward. He wanted to build up his chest muscles and be more attractive to girls. The fourth wanted to train for a charity bicycle rally in North Africa and the fifth wanted to become a fitness instructor.

Motivation and intention are not the same thing. Once the energy to actually *do* something is available, intention gives the necessary impulse to find direction. When we are clear about intention, it will create a pathway for action. If we can remember that energy follows thought and that thought is creative, then we have a fine motivation for refining and intensifying our intention.

Rupert Sheldrake, in his fascinating book *Dogs That Know When Their Owners Are Coming Home*,[3] gives convincing examples of how an owner's *intention* to do something, like feed the dog or cat, was picked up by the animal, who was some distance away. The animal would then appear within seconds from out of nowhere.

Sheldrake concludes, 'The evidence suggests that our own intentions, desires and fears are not just confined to our heads, or communicated only through words and behaviour.'[4] He is convinced that we can influence animals and affect other people at a distance, and that 'we can be influenced by things that are about to happen in ways that defy our normal notions of causality'.[5] He believes that we are at the threshold of a new understanding of the nature of mind.

Consider this for a moment: *our very thinking creates energy that goes in the direction of the thinking.* In other words, if we think about something or someone, we send powerful energy currents in that direction. This would suggest that an interconnection exists between two things that are separated in space and time. Sheldrake concludes that 'Animals have an ability that we have lost. One part of ourselves has forgotten this; another part has known it all along.'[6]

Our intentions focus energy like a beacon of light into a specific direction and set off responses, which frequently come in the form of synchronistic phenomena. For example in my practice people quite often discuss career problems. If it is a question of not having enough work and therefore not earning enough money, I ask them to write down how much they would like to earn. Then I ask them how many more orders or assignments this would take. They then consider how much more they can actually do within a day or week and how much more income that would generate. This produces results with remarkable speed. The process needs to be given serious attention and cannot be executed in a hurry. The very ritual of writing down what you want and what you are willing to give in return starts an unfolding of events. Try it out for yourself.

You can also make a much bigger plan – a ten-year plan, where you list *everything* you would like to have achieved ten years from now. Then you make a five-year plan, taking from the ten-year plan all those items that you think or feel are achievable in five. Then you do the same with a three- or two-year plan, a one-year plan and finally consider what you could achieve this week or even today. This form of planning works well and attracts synchronistic phenomena in great numbers. When I tried it out years ago I was astonished to discover, when looking at my ten-year plan only two years later, that I had achieved more than 80 per cent of my target. Such is the power of intention.

Synchronicities tell us that underlying our ordinary consciousness is an intelligent, creative and infinitely sensitive organizing pattern that defies and transcends individual understanding. When our intention is in earnest and when we imbue it with energy by focusing our thoughts and feelings and by visualizing the desired outcome, we generate a force that is truly creative and can usher in the future – as long as we heed the warning to be careful what we wish for, because we are sure to get it.

If we aim for the best, we will attract the best. The man who wanted to become a gym instructor intended to become the best. This meant that once he started his new career, he didn't just take individuals through an exercise routine, but also studied nutrition, counselling and any other subject that he felt could be useful in his work. Needless to say that in no time at all he had built up an impressive practice.

When I began studying astrology, my intention in the beginning was to learn as much as I could and to finish the course so that I could start the actual work and support myself. When I reached that goal my intention changed to becoming the best astrologer I could be. Later the intention changed again and so did the motivation. Both are fluid and change when our needs do.

A good policy, when we embark on any venture, is to ask ourselves, 'Whom does the Grail serve?' – in other words, what are we doing something *for*? If we are in it for the money, we need to ask ourselves what we want the money for and what *that* would give us. If you keep asking what something is for, you might just come to realize what you are *really* trying to create in your life. Money, for example, often symbolizes power, sex, happiness or freedom. That is why accumulating wealth usually does not bring the satisfaction that was originally sought.

PURPOSE

Our intentions, like synchronicities, are intimately interwoven with our purpose. Motivation without intent does not point anywhere. Discharging energy in random activity neither constitutes intent nor purpose. But when we are able, with intent, to connect to our purpose, each day assumes greater meaning and we realize that purpose is a mighty force.

Some people feel that our purpose is to feel happy 'at home' in ourselves, others to remember who we truly are. There is much talk today of our purpose being a conscious connection to other realms of existence, to worlds of other dimensions and vibrations, yet none the less worlds that form part of the one world. But in order to find out what our particular purpose in the large scheme of things is we need to connect with something tangible, something that gives us an idea of why we are here and how we can play our part, no matter how apparently small and insignificant, in moving things along.

It is difficult to talk about purpose in general terms because it is an individual quest. But one of the requirements that perhaps attaches to all purposes is the alignment of our small personal self with the soul; or, to put it another way, the alignment of our personal purpose with that of the soul's.

Let me give you an example. Alison, a woman in her forties, was a sculptor who felt that her reason for being was to sculpt. Most days she would be in her studio from dawn till dusk. All she knew was that she felt obsessively driven to sculpt. But then her relationship started to hit trouble. She simply had not enough time for it. When Ben, her husband, saw her in the evenings she would be exhausted and absent-minded and only talked about her work.

When we explored why she felt the need to carve and hammer and create various shapes over and over again from different angles and in different mediums, she finally reached the conclusion that she wanted to make the world a more beautiful place by showing nature's natural forms and shapes in all their glory. She smiled and said she remembered the story of the three stonecutters who were asked by a passer-by why they were cutting stone. The first one replied, 'I'm just cutting stones, can't you see?' The second replied, 'I am earning a living for my family.' But the third, beaming, with love in his eyes, said, 'I am building a great cathedral.' At this point Alison started crying softly. She understood that she wasn't going to win any Brownie points for working to the point of collapse and that creating beauty, building a great cathedral, is different from working for work's sake. Her newfound insight, simple as it may sound, had a tremendous effect on her and changed her relationship with Ben for the better.

Purpose is already encoded in our souls before we are born and therefore there is someone inside us who knows what it is. If you don't have a clue at all why you're here, watch synchronicities. If you feel that they don't happen to you, ask for them. But you'll have to turn your thinking on its head if you want to find out what they are supposed to mean. Keep on asking and then respond to them. Synchronicities are signposts to purpose. No matter how inert you may be on conscious levels, and how reluctant to change, there is someone inside you who will give you clues and keep on giving you clues.

We can also encourage the other to become a conscious reality in your lives by acting *as if* they were there with us in person. You could imagine, for instance, that you are asking the

Other questions and that you can hear the reply. Accept the first thing you hear. You may ask questions about anything you like. Some people find it easier to write the dialogue. It doesn't matter how you visualize the Other, in fact any image will do as long as it is supposed to represent a being of wisdom. In time you will be able to tell whether what is being said to you comes from your higher Self or some other source of wisdom or whether it comes from your little self and is only wishful thinking or criticism.

The unconscious, through dreams and synchronicities, will inform us of the next step we need to take. The problem is that many of us have a saboteur inside who wants to spoil things. This saboteur is often a voice of judgement. It questions everything we do and tells us that we don't amount to much. This is why it is so vital to be connected to purpose. This connection is stronger than the destructive little critical self. A true and committed connection to our chosen path, a path that we never tread for ourselves alone, will in the end override all doubt. When we feel that we are making a contribution to the creation of a better world, no matter how small, we *are* fulfilling our purpose.

We fulfil our immediate purpose in the little things that demand our attention every day. One way that some of the people I work with have found consistently useful is giving whatever they are doing their full attention, whether it is washing the dishes, creating a garden, writing a book or counselling a friend. Treating everything as if it were the most important thing brings purpose to even the smallest detail of our lives. In this way we act from the highest good. The secret of this way of living life is that you actually partake of the benefit of what you are creating, and in no mean measure. If at the same time you can also imagine that some form of higher intelligence is guiding you, the power and inspiration you are capable of invoking will increase immeasurably and enrich your life beyond your dreams, as well as building a bridge to another dimension.

NOTES

1 C. G. Jung, *Letters, 3/33*, Routledge & Kegan Paul, 1955.

2 Aniela Jaffé, *The Myth of Meaning*, G. P. Putnam's Sons, 1971.

3 Rupert Sheldrake, *Dogs That Know When Their Owners Are Coming Home*, Hutchinson, 1999.

4 Ibid.

5 Ibid.

6 Ibid.

KAIROS – THE NICK OF TIME

CHAPTER FIVE

We have no point of reference if we do not acknowledge time as being the primordial essence of the manifested universe – an essence which is sacred to all but the profane.

THEUN MARES

The word *kairos* comes from the Greek word meaning 'the right point in time' and also 'hitting the target'. *Kairos* is that gap between time and space where forces and circumstances flow together to create, out of their joint substance, something new. Time, space and physical reality blend together and the veil that normally separates the three disappears. At this point it is possible to catch a glimpse of the profound wholeness that underlies and informs our existence. In that moment, when time virtually 'shrinks to almost zero', as Jung put it,[1] it even becomes possible, with the right awareness, to take part in events in another dimension, as in lucid dreams and certain types of vision, out-of-the-body experiences and astral travelling. That is why synchronistic phenomena have something 'miraculous' about them. They make us sit up and marvel at what has just happened.

Another peculiar aspect of *kairos* is that it is no respecter of time sequence as we know it. For instance in dreams we often experience an event before it has happened. In these dreams the future is already happening. Does this mean that time is also then and now, here and in the past *and* in the future? Does it mean that a certain event has already happened in the future and that we are simply catching up with time? These are profound questions that no one as yet has been able to find answers for.

Time is a peculiar concept. We are used to living in Earth's 24-hour-a-day time capsule. But under certain circumstances time takes on an altogether different meaning. When you are waiting for something wonderful to happen, time goes on forever. When you are about to part from a lover, time flies. Sometimes, when we are working to a deadline, we are working against time. Then again, time can be against us if we only have a small amount available. The old proverb 'Time and tide wait for no man' seems to suggest that time has a will of its own, that it flows on like Old Man River, having witnessed all, yet, unconcerned, moving forward and onward.

We cannot save up time from our 24-hour day. When the day has gone the time has gone, too. In astrology the planet Saturn is known as Father Time because, as depicted by Goya in his famous painting, he eats his children, the minutes and seconds, as soon as they are born. The only way we can escape the tyranny of time is to live 'in time' or to be 'lost in time'. When you are truly and passionately involved in a particular activity, you lose the sense of time because you feel free of its constraints. Children for the most part still have this ability to be in step with time and hence lost in time, but alas, with increasing time demands put on them they, too, are fast losing this ability which is so necessary for creative activity.

The following anecdote powerfully illustrates modern time-travel. It concerns the Indian guru Sai Baba and his legendary ability to teleport himself, as well as others, vast distances. When a group of Australians was visiting him in India, one of them got a telegram informing him that his wife was gravely ill and might die. Baba assembled the group and by tapping on the wall produced a map of Australia. By repeatedly tapping the map he eventually produced an image of the man's front door. With one last tap the door opened and Baba beckoned the man to step through. He did and disappeared. The group phoned home and found out that he was indeed there. He had simply slipped through a nick in time and reached his destination by some unknown means. These accounts are hard to believe because we are trapped in an earthbound concept of space, time and matter. But as more and more people have such experiences they will eventually become an everyday occurrence.

Just over three years ago, when we were still living in London, something happened to give me a different understanding of time. It was a balmy summer's night and we had stayed up late in the garden talking to an old friend who had come to stay the night. When I finally went to bed I couldn't sleep, it was far too hot and my husband was tossing and turning. I put on a light dressing-gown, picked up a thin sheet and went down to the sitting room, where it was cooler, to sleep on the sofa.

About an hour later I was woken up by someone crouching next to me. 'Where is your handbag?' a voice whispered.

Half-awake, I thought it was our visitor and said, 'Go back to bed.'

The voice came sharper now, repeating the question. Suddenly I twigged. We had an intruder! I said, 'I haven't got a handbag.'

'Don't give me that, lady! Take me to your handbag.' He sounded fierce and threatening now.

I realized that this was serious and I needed to figure out the best plan of action. And time slowed down, miraculously! I was able to work out in my head, within no more than three seconds, all the various things I could do. I could take the intruder downstairs to where my handbag was, in the spare bedroom, where our friend was sleeping. But I decided that he would be no help at all, that he had probably had too much to drink and would be fast asleep by now. The other option was to take him upstairs to our bedroom, hoping that my husband would wake and protect me.

I became extremely calm, got up and said, 'It's upstairs.' He twisted my right arm behind my back and said, 'Don't turn the light on or make a sound or I'll slit your throat.'

I walked steadily up the stairs. When we reached the upper landing he tried to divert me from our bedroom, but I insisted that my handbag was in there. I opened the door, switched on the light and said firmly, 'Ean, we have an intruder in the house.' And Ean, who was lying stark naked across the bed, opened his eyes and without a moment's reflection jumped up with a war cry and went for the culprit, who had just enough time to cry out, 'Now you've done it!' before he ran down the two flights of stairs at lightning speed and disappeared into the night.

It was not until the police arrived and asked me if I needed a counsellor that I realized that I had never for one moment been afraid and had felt that I could take all the time I needed to make the right decision in this emergency.

A couple of nights previously my husband had dreamed that a ferret was trying to get into our house to get at our two cats. He didn't like the dream, but we couldn't figure out what it meant until after the intruder had been in, when he remembered that the French word for ferret is *furet* and signifies 'someone who sniffs around'. Maybe the intruder was a 'sniffer' of some kind of substance and was after money to feed his habit.

Many people have had the experience of time stretching or expanding. It is such a well-known occurrence that everyone knows that when we see a slow-motion scene in a film the director is seeking to portray that extraordinary dimension of time. Our dreams also sometimes contain such scenes.

I first heard about this stretch in time from my first therapist. She had done her professional psychotherapy training in

America in the 1960s and it was not uncommon then for her teacher to administer small doses of LSD to his students in order to facilitate, intensify and accelerate transpersonal and/or numinous experiences. On one occasion she had been given double the dose as her teacher thought it might give her deeper insight into the paranoid feelings she was experiencing at times. As a result she entered into what she described as an altogether different world of indescribable beauty. Here she spent what she thought were the next couple of days. The experience itself was the most extraordinary she had ever had and was full of wonders and colours and strange people with strange messages.

When she returned to normal clock time and learnt that only a few minutes had elapsed, her mind could not deal with this apparent dichotomy. She became so disoriented that she went 'mad' for several weeks. During this period she experienced acute and horrifying paranoia and was in a state of perpetual and relentless terror. She was unable to function and spent most of the time in bed, curled up in a ball. Eventually the gap closed, the feelings subsided and she returned to 'normal' reality once more. But from that time on she knew, so she told me, what paranoia truly was, and especially what her own persecution complex was all about. For this reason she has never regretted the experiment.

I believe that time is magical, as are the devices with which we measure it. Clocks stop at strange times and at others, miraculously, start working again. Sometimes we mistakenly think it is one time when it is another. Many of us have had experiences of alarm clocks going off too soon or too late or not at all and thereby making us miss trains, planes or buses and experience significant consequences as a result.

A few years ago I did some research into the well-known phenomenon of the stopping of watches at crucial turning points in people's lives. What I discovered was very interesting. Without exception I found that when someone's watch broke and could not be mended, a cycle in that person's life had come to an end. They moved house, changed jobs or partners, or made other significant changes. For instance, the day my son Andrew graduated from university, his wristwatch stopped working. He took it to be mended but was told that it was not worth repairing and he threw it away. As he walked home he found a better watch on a window sill and took it as a signal that better times now lay ahead. Research also shows that quite often when people enter prison their watches stop working as they cross the threshold.

The apparently autonomous behaviour of clocks and watches is fascinating. Just yesterday I fixed my bathroom clock. Its battery had run out weeks ago. As it hangs in an awkward place that can only be reached with a ladder I kept putting off replacing it. But because I had clocks and watches and time on my mind I needed to do something about it. Besides, I was curious to discover whether mending clocks would make things move more quickly. Thirty minutes later a newspaper telephoned, offering me a substantial writing project. You may call this a chance happening, but to me the two events took on synchronistic significance. But try the experiment for yourself and see what happens.

Examples of synchronicity concerning other inanimate objects, like books falling off shelves and cars going wrong at crucial moments, abound, but watch stories are the best known and the most common. Now, when a watch stops, I never take it lightly and either get it fixed right away or throw it out. In fact I would advise anyone to do the same, because symbolically a time piece that does not work suggests that one is suspended in time and nothing moves.

The stopping of clocks and watches is a frequently observed phenomenon at the time of death. Several years ago I went with my friend Charles Harvey to the house of a man who had recently died and who had bequeathed his library to the Astrological Association. Charles was President of the Association at the time, and I turned up late one night at this very sombre-looking house in a suburb of London. The man's wife had died a few months earlier and in his grief he had painted every wall, door and window frame black. Whilst Charles was busy talking to someone about the books, I sat quietly and waited. During this time I was able to observe that every clock in the room – and there were four – had stopped at 5.40. Later, when we were on our way with a car full of books, I asked Charles if the time of death was known. 'Yes, of course, it was 5.40 in the morning.' He had not noticed the clocks himself but was impressed none the less.

There is a poignant postscript to this story. The night after writing about this particular incident, I dreamed that I had two watches and that they had both stopped at 2.50. I didn't like the dream and explained it away by the fact that I had just written about death and the synchronistic phenomenon of the stopping of clocks. But a couple of days later came the sad news that Charles had died – at 2.50 a.m. the night I had the dream!

Animals can also display uncanny behaviour around the time of a death. One of the most moving examples was told me by David Cairns, a friend of mine, who had observed his West Highland terrier, Amos, licking his cat, Malachi, all over, while the normally very frisky cat stood stock still. This had never happened before. The odd 'grooming' continued for 'a very long time'. David was puzzled, but then paid it no more attention. The significance became clear early the next day when the cat was hit by a passing car and died a few hours afterwards. Although we don't know what prompted the dog to be so affectionate towards the cat, it would appear that at some level he *knew* that his friend would soon depart and so prepared him for the journey and said goodbye.

Another example involves a bird who knew the right time. My husband and I had recently moved onto a houseboat. We were sitting peacefully on deck when a seagull flew rather lamely onto the roof and sat there with what appeared to be a broken wing. It looked very sick. We tried to frighten it away, clapping our hands and waving our arms, but it would not budge. It sat there for most of the day with one wing hanging down off the roof. Then, just as suddenly as it had come, it stood up, shook itself, gave a haunting cry and flew off with perfectly strong wings. The next day came the news that my husband's brother Gordon had died unexpectedly in the early hours of the morning.

Aniela Jaffé[2] gives a number of examples where even plants mirror an inner event, as when someone dies and the plant follows suit. She has also observed that synchronistic phenomena increase around a death. These can include a bright flash of light, a beautiful smell or the mysterious sounds of angelic music. Shamans believe – or know? – that death is simply walking from one room to another. But because most of us do not yet understand death and what happens afterwards, we tend to be frightened rather than feeling privileged at being chosen to be witness to the second most important experience of our lives after birth.

Perhaps the old proverbs 'There is a time for everything' and 'There is a time to live and a time to die' suggest that the moment, the *kairos*, of death is more fixed and predictable than we might care to consider. It is my belief that in situations of mortal danger, when it is *not* the right moment to die, Fate, or synchronicity, steps in to change the course of events.

Another aspect of *kairos*, von Franz reminds us,[3] is associated with goddesses who 'weave time'. In this sense we think of time as a vast network of interwoven threads whose nodal points are the meaningful coincidences which interconnect the whole tapestry. That is one of the reasons why I believe that synchronistic events are never isolated happenings, for they are linked by an unseen chain of events. Von Franz thought that synchronicities became more numerous when a gradient of energy existed between an individual's conscious and unconscious, as when we are in a state of high emotional excitement.

Many years ago I had a chain of unusual synchronistic experiences which demonstrate exactly this point. It was at the beginning of my relationship with my husband. We had been apart for most of the summer. He was driving back from Switzerland and we had arranged to meet on the other side of the English Channel, in Ostend. The weather forecast the night before had announced severe gales, but I had paid no attention to it and drove to Dover early the next morning. The port was in total chaos. People were sitting, standing and lying down everywhere. There were no ferries leaving for Ostend until further notice. I stood calmly for a moment, wondering what to do next. I could not imagine us not meeting up that day. Then I heard an announcement, though unfortunately it was not for my ferry but for the only one that day to Calais! Without thinking, I ran as fast as I could for the Calais ferry and just managed to jump onto the car-deck as the ramp was being pulled up.

I found a seat and relaxed – for a while. But what now? I sent a message to my unconscious mind to come up with a solution and a few seconds later I knew what to do. I went to the bathroom, brushed my hair, put some make-up on, then climbed the steep steps to the top deck to see the radio officer. Putting on all the charm I could muster, I told him that I needed to get to Ostend that day for an important meeting. Would he please make an announcement over the loudspeaker for anyone who was driving from Calais to Ostend to come to Information? He obliged without hesitation, happy to be of service. And there was indeed someone, a jolly man who was driving to Leipzig, to the toy fair, via Ostend. Two other people also asked for a ride. Before I left the ferry I embraced the radio officer warmly, kissed him on the cheek and thanked him. 'Just for that,' he chuckled, 'it was worth it!'

I had an enjoyable journey to my destination in very pleasant company, but when I arrived in Ostend I was faced with the problem of finding Ean. I had no idea which hotel he would have booked us into and as it was midday the tourist office was closed. I told the taxi driver that I wanted to check the big hotels on the waterfront as I had an uncanny feeling that he would have chosen somewhere with a sea view. Unbelievably, the second hotel we tried was the right one, but Ean had gone to the port to look for me. I set off after him and found the port in as much a chaos as Dover. No ferries had arrived and none were leaving. Hundreds of people were milling about. I looked around for a while but then gave up and I was about to return to the hotel when I heard someone call my name. I turned around and saw Ean's head sticking out of a telephone box. Our meeting was one of those magical moments when you cannot believe that something is actually real and you keep pinching yourself. To complete this synchronistic chain of events, the person Ean had been talking to on the telephone the very moment he spotted me was the hotel receptionist, asking whether by any chance I had turned up!

Von Franz would say that it was our heightened emotional state that made us tune into archetypal forces and thus elicit a chain of synchronicities. I feel that by trusting the right thing to turn up, by refusing to be defeated when our instincts and intuition tell us to plough on, we increase our chances of letting synchronicity step in and see us through.

NOTES

1 C. G. Jung, *Synchronicity: An Acausal Connecting Principle*, Routledge & Kegan Paul, 1955.

2 Aniela Jaffé, *Apparitions*, Spring Publications, 1978.

3 Marie-Louise von Franz, *Number and Time*, Rider, 1974.

THE PROMISE OF COINCIDENCE

CHAPTER SIX

A warrior relaxes and abandons himself; he fears nothing. Only then will the powers that guide human beings open the road for a warrior and aid him. Only then.

CARLOS CASTANEDA

The promise of synchronicity is that of a life more abundant. Synchronistic events remind us that another, altogether different order of reality is intelligently operating on our behalf. This is a sign that an interconnectedness exists in far wider measure than we may have thought possible. If we are indeed all part of an unimaginably vast world, then it would stand to reason that our potential is similarly vast. There is much talk nowadays of the ancient Akashic records, which are said to contain the collective and individual memories of the human family. Remembering who we are as part of the one world promises a release from illusion – the imprisoning constraints of matter – and the opportunity to become conscious souls. At least that is the theory.

Whether this is so or not I do not know; however, with a little daily observation, we can all learn about the Other, as already mentioned, and can work towards finding our true vocation. Although we are all in 'a common flow, a common breathing, in sympathy with all, with a common purpose', as Hippocrates said,[1] we all have our own purpose and destiny. So it follows that my synchronicity is not the same as yours. When I see a coin lying in the road, I pick it up, knowing that good news is on its way, but for Michael Ondaatje, author of *The English Patient*, it is pins. His motto is 'See a pin and pick it up, and all the day you'll have good luck.' Even when he is smartly dressed for dinner and out walking with friends, he will pick up some filthy pin, his insurance policy for continued success. A concert pianist I know picks up small shiny objects and leaves and petals, and assembles them into beautiful pictures. It started out as a therapeutic exercise, but then became an artistic vocation. Of course, synchronistically, she finds the most amazing bits and pieces, like tiny items of fine jewellery, delicate glass marbles and pearls, that seem to have been dropped by fairies in flight. For each one of us, the language of synchronicity is unique and only we can decipher it. But, at the same time, synchronicity also promises that the more attention you pay to it, the luckier you get.

When we begin to observe synchronistic phenomena, respond to their flirting and follow their promptings, we commence the conscious process of soul-making. We learn to discern what is synchronicity and what is not. We learn to wait and see what the meaning might be, and also learn to act immediately if the occasion demands. If we honour synchronistic phenomena we will notice quickly how our consciousness widens and how our responses to life situations become more certain and more flexible.

Whilst it is not possible to pre-arrange meaningful coincidences, there are methods by which we can become more aware of them. The most obvious one is to learn to live in the here and now, as if this were the last day of your life. Try to notice everything that is going on around you. Pay attention to your dreams *(see Chapter 7)* and the thoughts you wake up with. I have found that invariably my early-morning thoughts tell me what I must do that day, what I forgot to do the day before and what mistakes I have made that need correcting. Only this morning I woke up with the thought that I should not send a letter I had written the night before. When I picked up the envelope I noticed that I had forgotten to include the number and name of the street and write the return address on the back.

Another way to become more present in the moment is to meditate. I don't just mean sitting in silence and trying not to think of anything, focusing on a candle or listening to the voice of the silence, but intense concentration which leads to the awakening of dormant brain cells. For this one is better off in a meditation school for instruction, such as the Arcane School, which has its headquarters in London, Geneva and

New York. However, this work is not for the faint-hearted and demands regular study, dedication and persistence.

Learning to read Tarot cards can also awaken the intuition if one treats the cards as a form of meditation and not just as a game or a means of foretelling the future *(see Chapter 9)*.

Intense meditation that serves to strengthen and purify thought processes will also increase synchronistic phenomena and prepare us for the next stage of our journey. Then, when someone is ready to work with higher energies, it will happen naturally.

In the meantime just be aware of the smallest signs of progress. If you think of a friend and a half hour later she telephones, congratulate yourself. You have either sent out your intention and she received it, or you picked up hers. We can also invite synchronicities by wishing for something or by thinking strongly enough about a certain thing, for the veil that separates us from the Otherworld is thinner than we know. My friend the opera singer Thomas Hemsley recently told me what happened to him 11 years ago:

I decided that the time was becoming ripe for me to retire from public singing. I said to my wife Gwen, 'There are two works that I would dearly love to sing once more before I retire: Vaughan Williams's *Sea Symphony* and Delius's *Sea Drift*. Many years ago I used to sing these works, which were very close to my heart, but I can't imagine that anyone would ask me to sing either of these at this stage in my career.'

About 10 days later I received a letter from Aarhus Symphony Orchestra in Denmark asking if I would be interested in singing at a concert which consisted of *both these works*. It proved to be my last orchestral concert.

Smells can also trigger a synchronistic connection. I was walking down the King's Road in Chelsea last week. It was 12.30 p.m. and I was taking my lunch break. As I passed Whittard's coffee shop, the aroma was enticing. It reminded me of my friend Ann, whom I was staying with at the time, because she always makes the most delicious coffee in the morning. All at once I thought of the time when Ann tripped over her cats and fell and broke her thigh in two places. She lay in her hall for ages, not being able to move or reach the telephone, before someone came, then spent weeks in hospital. The fractures took many months to heal. She is now well again, but I am sure that such an experience caused her unimaginable suffering. Suddenly I felt a deep and unexpected compassion for my friend. That night I told her about it and mentioned the time that I had those thoughts. She smiled, not at all surprised, and said, 'That was the exact moment when I entered St James's Palace and stumbled over a rug in the hall, and I was terrified that I might have broken something again!'

Is it possible that we are connected to other people via a 'world wide web' and perhaps our concerns about them summon help to protect them? It is my firm belief that the Internet is the forerunner of collective consciousness and that it is only a matter of time before our brains have developed the capacity to make those links consciously. Sheldrake cites many incidences where people or animals know of the danger someone else is in and get help at the right time.[2]

It can also happen that we get the sense that someone is *not* in danger when everyone else thinks they are. Shelly, a busy psychotherapist and caring mother of three grown-up children, was telephoned once in the middle of the night by a hospital nurse saying that her son, aged 24 and at university at the time, had been admitted with a possible brain haemorrhage and that they would give him a scan in the morning. He was disorientated and couldn't remember who or where he was. Shelly remained perfectly calm and told the nurse that she would not come that night but the next day, around noon, when she had finished her morning's work. She had no sense of urgency or danger. His sisters, however, were very upset when their mother telephoned them the next morning and dropped everything and rushed to his bedside.

When Shelly eventually went to see her son she found a pale and confused young man, but still did not get a feeling that there was anything really wrong with him. What did disturb her, however, was that the ward was filthy and very noisy. She did not feel that she could subject her son to such conditions and, so, the following day, when they had still not started the promised tests, she took him home and managed to get an appointment with a kinesiologist who also happened to be an osteopath. About two hours later he returned, cheerful and laughing and back to his normal self. A nerve had become trapped in his neck and was numbing other nerves. One twist of the neck and it had been released. Something inside Shelly had known all along that her son was safe.

Noticing the signs along the way can not only lead you out of danger, but even get you a parking space where none is to be had. Here is an example where synchronicity saved the day. We were in Sicily, in an extremely busy seaside town below Taormina. Our hotel was overlooking the sea and a road separated it from the beach. It was a Saturday and we had been out looking at Holy Grail sites all day. When we returned in the evening we were horrified to see that all the roads were congested with hundreds of cars and there was not a parking space in sight. We would have to park somewhere outside the town. Lying on top of my bag was a picture of the Indian avatar Mother Meera.[3] I looked at her and she smiled back calmly. How could I forget that when she travelled with us she invoked synchronicities? As we approached the hotel, there, as if surrounded by an invisible force field, was an empty parking space outside the hotel – the same one we had parked in the night before.

This may be an example of rather minor importance, but we have had numerous similar occurrences while travelling which have made an enormous difference to our comfort and well-being. Over the years we have come to admit that there is a mysterious Other who looks out for us and points us in the right direction. In my view it is a question of reading the signs and laying aside scepticism and, above all, cynicism. Synchronicity cannot enter where these two rule. If we want to benefit from otherworldly intelligence and protection, we need to open ourselves fully to all that is possible – and to what seems impossible. Trust is the key – trust that the right thing will turn up and that there is someone taking care of us, especially in times of danger. *That* is the promise of synchronicity.

NOTES

1 Jung quoting Hippocrates in *Synchronicity: An Acausal Connecting Principle*, Routledge & Kegan Paul, 1955.

2 Rupert Sheldrake, *Dogs That Know When Their Owners Are Coming Home*, Hutchinson, 1999.

3 *See* Andrew Harvey, *The Inner Journey*, Century, 1992.

THE STUFF OF DREAMS

CHAPTER SEVEN

The art of dreaming is the capacity to utilize one's ordinary dreams and transform them into controlled awareness by virtue of a specialised form of attention called the dreaming attention.

CARLOS CASTANEDA

Dreams are one of the most common sources of synchronistic phenomena. During sleep ordinary consciousness 'goes to sleep', giving the unconscious a chance to break through and speak. Like synchronicities, the dream mind seems to have knowledge of a higher and different order of intelligence.

Although it may appear much of the time that dreams are only about everyday humdrum things, this is in fact far from the truth. Dreams will take images and experiences from our daily lives – for this is the stuff they work with – but will transform them into profound messages from the unconscious. The communications we receive in dream states are always something that *we do not already know*, but should, something that applies to our lives *now*.

It takes practice to decipher the many different layers of dreams correctly, but the effort we make in paying attention to them will be well rewarded with deeper insights into our lives and those of others. Dreams and synchronicities *promise* something. This becomes apparent when one has been analysing one's dreams for some time. Nightmare figures turn into heroes, the chase into a warm kiss, the cripple into a god.

The more we become interested in our dreams, the more they will communicate with us. For this reason it is always a good idea to have a notepad and pen handy in order to write them down on waking. Dreams are elusive and if we don't catch them early they can evaporate in no time at all like a delicate mist. Sometimes we will remember them during the day but we can't rely on it. Even if you do not understand your dreams at the time, the act of writing them down shows a commitment and your dream mind is aware of that. If you then carry your dreams around with you in your pocket, so to speak, you might just catch the meaning in a flash of inspiration.

When I was going through my own Jungian analysis, which focused mainly on my dreams, they came hard and fast at the rate of six or seven every night. I would wake up, write them down and go back to sleep immediately, as if my body and mind knew that I was sleeping in order to dream. The unconscious mind had become activated and once that happens it reveals, in the most amazing colours, symbols and images, a world of which most of the time we are totally unaware.

Dreams are a perfect system for monitoring our own individuation process, that is, our personal unfolding, for whatever we are is hidden within their stories and pictures. They will also keep an eye on our relationships and their development, and will warn us if need be. Paying attention to such a warning can save a great deal of time and energy. I was once having a light-hearted relationship with a lovely man. He was a Steve McQueen lookalike and reminded me of the type of guy I had fancied when I was in my teens. As time went by he became more and more attached to me and fantasized about setting up home together. I wouldn't say that I was in love with him, but I found him attractive and intelligent enough. We had a lot of fun together and our relationship was not without passion. But I kept dreaming of him being sick – he would either have an eye missing or be a bedridden cripple. Although these dreams made me feel uneasy, I could not grasp their meaning and for that reason gave them little attention.

Then one day he told me about his visitations from people from outer space and that he had been planted on planet Earth to help save it. Now, it is not that I don't believe that there are other realities and other worlds apart from ours, far from it, but the way he related these happenings to me, made them sound more like delusions than real contact with extra-terrestrials. One day he asked me to have a special garment made, a loose white robe that I was to wear on special occasions, and he would have it blessed by the priest of Southwark cathedral in London. I had just had another of those dreams in which he needed medical help and therefore took this latest event as a sign to quit the relationship. I haven't seen him since. He came into my life in a flash and left just as quickly. Had it not been for my dreams I would probably not have realized so soon he had something wrong with him. There is nothing wrong with visitations – many of us have them, either in dreams or in waking consciousness – but it was the *tone* of the dream that gave me the vital information I needed to know.

I have often wondered why dreams give us insight into future events that are not particularly important. Sometimes we dream that we receive a letter from a friend and the next morning there it is on our doormat. Sometimes we dream of a political event that actually happens very shortly after. Occasionally I have dreamed about next day's weather. Sometimes this is useful, of course. Before I was going on a trip to Spain at Easter, when the temperatures are normally very high, I dreamed that I should take a warm sweater. Sure enough, we made an excursion to the Pyrenees, where there was still snow on the ground and the air very cool.

If we pay close attention to our dreams we begin to realize that the same Other that speaks to us through synchronicities also speaks to us in dreams. Dreams and synchronicities are both for our own good. Even when they frighten us, they are trying to show that something is wrong and needs fixing. Jung said that we must respond to the dream and engage with it. By that he meant that we must reflect on it and investigate further. A dream's message is often obscure; that is because dreams have to portray their message in pictorial and symbolic language. Having a dream is like watching a movie – often a silent movie.

The French talk about 'making' a dream, which is perhaps more accurate than 'having' a dream. Dreams are carefully constructed works of art, a magically interwoven tapestry. The dream mind conveys a message with the material available as best it can. As well as images and ideas from our everyday life, it can include archetypal images such as God, the Great Mother, angels, aliens and devils, to name but a few. Dreams containing such images always have a numinous quality about them. They cannot be interpreted in terms of everyday events. They need another kind of approach altogether because they are messages from the deepest inner realms that cannot be reached via ordinary consciousness. Sometimes we simply need to live with these dreams for a while until we realize what they are about. Numinous and archetypal dreams are concerned with the soul's evolution and this usually unfolds quite independently of what is happening in our outer world. For this reason it is advisable to seek the help of someone who knows how to work with dream symbolism, such a therapist familiar with Jung's work.

RECURRING DREAMS

Dreams and synchronicity are intimately bound up with one another. If we don't get it first time round the message will be repeated until we do, or until the psyche finds we are a hopeless case and gives up on us. It is of vital importance therefore that recurring dreams are listened to. The very fact that they come again and again points to their urgency.

When I had no idea what I wanted to do with my life, I kept dreaming again and again about missing the boat, the train or the bus (this was in the early sixties when air travel was not that common). These dreams continued for months and months. Then, the night before the onset of my remarkable and frightening night sea journey *(see Chapter 4)*, I had a synchronistic dream: a large planet was travelling towards Earth with tremendous speed and hit it. The Earth split open and from its interior there poured forth a thick stream of golden coins. Of course I had no idea what it meant at the time, but in the dream it felt as if it was me who was splitting open, on the *inside*. Looking back, my terrifying experience proved to be of inestimable value, although at the time I would have preferred to die. My dream was telling me clearly and dramatically, in pictorial symbolism, that my world as I knew it was about to be violently destroyed, but that something of far greater value would flow from this split.

PROPHETIC DREAMS

Many dreams have a prophetic quality about them and often they are announcements of important future events such as death, birth or illness. The psyche seems to know well in advance when something tremendous is going to happen. Why it may want us to know certain things ahead of time remains a philosophical and metaphysical mystery. However, it would seem that on a psychic level the event has already occurred.

About 20 years ago I was in Germany for a visit and one of my sisters asked me if I would read the Tarot cards for her. This was my second oldest sister and the only one of us five who was still childless. After several miscarriages she had given up hope of ever conceiving again. The Tarot spread showed clearly that something extremely happy and joyous was about to happen. I was worried about giving my sister false hope and only dared to say to her that *if* she got pregnant again she would have the child and it would be exactly what she wanted. In view of her history I wasn't very optimistic and wondered whether the cards had simply picked up an extremely strong wish of hers.

This was in November. The following June I sent her a birthday card with a note saying that her present would follow soon. I got a letter back by return with the message that I should save up the present for late October because that is when her baby was due. At the time of the Tarot reading she had not yet become pregnant and for quite a while after conception had had no idea that she was pregnant. When she finally found out, in the fourth month, and told my father, he informed her that he had known for several months. He told her that in January, shortly after she had conceived, she had come to him in a dream and said that she was pregnant, and then she had placed a finger over her lips and said, 'But sshhh, don't tell anyone yet.' So he didn't.

Some dreams are of great importance, while others seem meaningless. We just shrug our shoulders, wonder what they were all about and pay no further attention to them. Yet, after many years of working with dreams I have come to realize that it is often in the fine detail that the clue to a dream's meaning is to be found. At other times it is only when we take the dream as a total *Gestalt*, as a complete picture, that we understand it.

A friend once asked me if I knew anyone who wanted to buy her house. It wasn't selling, although it was in a desirable area of London. She was getting desperate because she had already found the house she wanted to buy and didn't want to lose it. I told her what a Catholic American friend once said, that you should place a blessed statue of St Joseph in the window if you want to sell your property. She said she would do it immediately. That night I dreamed of a house that in the dream I knew belonged to her, which was actually physically moving. I telephoned her the following day and confidently announced that she would be moving very soon and not to worry. She did sell her house not long after my dream and several more synchronicities were involved in the process.

It is my belief that life is far more interconnected at all levels than we could imagine and that synchronicities, in a curious sense, are quite logical and occur in far greater numbers than we care to know. When we realize that an underlying life-pattern can reveal itself through them, and that sometimes this is the *only* way it can do so, we will find out how destructive and separating impatience and lack of trust are, and learn to follow the signs along the way.

ASTROLOGY – A MEANINGFUL COINCIDENCE

CHAPTER EIGHT

Whatever is born at a particular moment in time takes on the quality of that moment in time. The meaningful coincidence we are looking for is immediately apparent in astrology...

C. G. JUNG

Astrology is essentially the purest presentation of occult truth in the world at this time.

ALICE A. BAILEY

The synchronicity inherent in astrology is one of the most striking examples of a hidden order of reality. A horoscope, from the Greek *hora*, 'time', and *skopos*, 'observer', is a map of a moment in time. It is a graphic replica of how the sun, moon and planets were positioned around the Earth at a given moment. As this moment relates to something specific, e.g., the birth of a human being, it is a *synchronistic* one. The heavens are fluid and forever changing. Each moment is unique; the heavens will never repeat exactly the same pattern again. So, when someone is born the planetary pattern prevailing in the cosmos at that moment is also unique. Even identical twins born only a minute apart have their own blueprint. In fact exciting recent research shows that there are many instances where so-called 'identical' twins are genetically not identical at all – their DNA is different.

Each moment also has a *memory*. Every astrologer knows this. For instance, when you set up an individual birthchart for someone it becomes an entity in its own right. We can read the chart forward (some astrologers read it also backward to before birth) and predict what is going to happen at certain points in the future. This is not because astrologers are psychic – most often they are not – but for two other reasons. One is that our solar system is in constant flux. These changes affect us all the time because we are part of the greater cosmos and are subject to its laws.

The other reason is that in the complicated system of zodiacal signs, planets and houses each has a specific meaning that the skilled and intuitive astrologer can interpret. So, when a planet on its journey around the sun comes to a point in the ecliptic where another planet was positioned when we were born, it is of great significance. The interpretation depends on the planet that was positioned there at birth and on the nature of the planet that has now arrived at this point. It doesn't take any skill to figure out that the planet that was there at birth has moved on and is now no longer there. This point has become just another degree on the ecliptic, like any other. So why then is it so significant when a planet comes to this empty degree? The curious fact is that the 'wandering stars', as the ancients used to call planets, will interact *as if that planet were still there.* In other words, that particular degree point has a memory, a memory that is unique, but only to the individual to whom the horoscope applies. It can remember that at a particular moment in time a certain heavenly body was positioned there.

For example, Venus, the planet of loving relationships, was in 28 degrees of Sagittarius when I was born. The planet Saturn, signifying separation and pain, would arrive at that point when I was 45. From this an astrologer could predict that I would have a painful experience involving a loved one at that time, because that is the nature of events when these two planets combine.

What happened to me then was that my husband and I had travelled by car from London to Italy to attend a conference that was opening at the Scuola de San Rocco in Venice and then continuing in Sesto, in the Dolomite mountains. We had carefully mapped out our journey so that we could visit a few places we had never been to. On the second day of our travels I realized that I had miscalculated the dates and we found, to our delight, that we had an extra day and two nights with no planned activities. We booked in to a beach hotel on the Adriatic Sea and spent the next day just hanging out, swimming, reading and having a long lunch.

Before dressing for dinner we went for a final swim. The beach had emptied, which meant that we could have the whole sea to ourselves. I was enjoying the warm soft water, floating on my back and soaking up the last rays of sun, when without warning, I became extremely frightened and found myself fighting for breath, convinced that I was going to drown. I had floated into a bed of seaweed whose gentle tentacles were curling around my limbs like tiny snakes, creating the sensation that I was about to be dragged under at any moment. I started to panic and fight off the engulfing 'arms'. My struggle seemed to go on forever, but eventually, deeply shaken, I reached the beach and collapsed on the sand.

This event was of a most unusual nature. I am not given to panic attacks and haven't had another one since. The following day we continued our journey. On the second night in Sesto, when we were just about to go to sleep, the telephone rang. It was my son calling from London. He had been trying to reach me for two days to tell me that my father had died unexpectedly. This came as a dreadful shock as I had loved him deeply.

The following morning we drove to Innsbruck to catch a plane to attend the funeral in Hamburg. As it was a rather long drive we turned on the radio and I immediately recognized the music: old shanties transmitted directly from the port of Hamburg. This had been my father's favourite music and when someone played *La Paloma* on a mouth-organ, I had to stop the car and give full vent to my emotions. He used to play this tune to my sisters and me when we were young, and only shortly before his death, during the filming of a documentary about the ship he was an officer on during World War II, he had played it on TV on his own old mouth organ. The music was followed by an interview with an American professor of nuclear physics called Paul Frackowiak, *the same name as my father's!* Hearing that music and then my father's name straight afterwards was a gift I received just at the right time. It was as if my father was saying his own special farewell to me. And, as all synchronicities do, it brought home once again the powerful message that there is an implicit order underlying all things. It also added to the beauty and poignancy of the Saturn conjunction with the 'remembered' Venus on my birthchart, and to my sadness and sense of loss.

Whilst in Hamburg we experienced more synchronicities, but it was only after we returned to London that I could check the tables of planetary positions. I discovered that my panic attack in the sea had happened at the precise moment of my father's death and that I had received my son's phone call when Saturn had been on exactly the same degree as Venus had been when I was born. Some of the interpretations for this configuration are unhappiness in love, separation, loss, sadness and bereavement. Others speak of love-unions with an appreciable age difference and the ability to make sacrifices for other people (we had to forego almost the entire conference, which was over by the time we returned to Innsbruck to collect our car). The Saturn–Venus connection means also a sense of duty and thrift and economy. This was borne out in our case by the fact that our insurance paid for all our travel costs and conference fees.

Seen in this way, then, every moment in time has the potential for memory. Each one of my children's birth moments, for instance, and their accompanying planetary positions in the ecliptic, meaningfully coincided with certain degrees on my own birthchart, as if some great intelligence had already determined the timing of these events at the moment of *my* birth. When my son was born, Venus was at the exact point where Jupiter had been at my birth and Jupiter itself was now passing over the degree where Venus had been at my birth. Astrologically, this combination signifies a great love between two people. Similar connections exist between my horoscope and those of my daughters. The same can be said of the comparisons of children's birthcharts with that of their fathers, siblings and even grandparents and other members of the family.

Every astrologer knows of the amazing synchronicities found between the birthcharts of people who have a significant relationship with one another. Jung even went so far as to conduct an extensive experiment, analysing the horoscopes of 180 married couples. He found significant correlations and made this research a central part of his book *Synchronicity*. Jung was very interested in astrology and knew far more about the subject than he let on. He considered the birthchart as a mirror of our fate, the hand we were dealt from the outset of life.

The synchronicity inherent in astrology is intimately connected with our lives and fates, and provides us, from birth, with a blueprint that indicates the kind of person we can be and the type of journey we need to make in order to realize this potential. Throughout life we are then given hints and chances, again and again and again, in the form of synchronistic events, which frequently correspond to the movements of the planets.

I don't want to give the impression that the birthchart says you are like this or that and that therefore you cannot change yourself. In fact, I am stating the opposite. The birthchart speaks of our *potential*, of what we can become if we develop fully. Character is something that we can grow into and change, although its basic traits probably need to be present from the very beginning. This reminds me of the axiom that if you change your present you will also change your future. Astrology can show up certain crucial developmental nodal points when changes are not only possible but also necessary.

Therefore the individual birthchart promises a life more abundant. It also promises that we are not separate from the larger cosmos, but on the contrary, very much an integral part of it, and that we should try and live in accordance with its laws.

The curious thing is that as soon as one understands another fragment of one's own being, a synchronistic event is waiting to happen. On the fateful day that I first encountered astrology, the planet that rules astrology, Uranus, and the planet of good fortune and opportunity, Jupiter, were in a positive angular relationship to one another. This combination is well known to astrologers as the 'lucky chance' and also as the 'Thank the Lord' aspect. It is so called because the combined action of these two giants often triggers a lucky break or a release from tension and pressure. On my birthchart, this configuration tied in neatly with the position of my Moon, which after the Sun is the most important factor on the chart. That day I experienced the most life-changing synchronistic phenomenon ever, and an enthusiastic and dedicated astrologer was born.

Astrologers will frequently consult a table of planetary positions in order to determine a good time for a particular event. I usually forget to do so, but have found again and again that the right circumstances seem to contrive to create a tapestry of such intricate detail that not even the best astrologer in the world could have improved upon it. Planetary influences weave their magic for us whether we are aware of it or not and connect us intimately with synchronicity. I would even go so far to say that in many respects (certainly in the *timing* of events), they are one and the same.

Whenever a major astrological event occurs it sets a new chain of cause and effect in motion. If we respond to the synchronicity of astrology with timely action we have the opportunity to begin a whole new life cycle.

Many people visit an astrologer because they are stuck, unhappy, bored, frightened or without direction and purpose. Having a birthchart analysed at such times can be a life-altering event. The astrologer sits there with a piece of paper and reads the strange markings and symbols on it as if reading a story from a book. He or she will tell you about your relationship with your parents and siblings, your attitude to learning, your particular talents and the areas where you need to make more effort, as well as many things about yourself that you didn't know and that at first you will have difficulty accepting. Fortunately, most chart readings nowadays are taped, and as you listen to the tape over and over again, you will become familiar with this bigger picture of yourself. As you begin to become aware of what you are in potential, synchronicities will start rolling in with great urgency and frequency, demanding your attention.

It is very common for someone to have a chart reading and then to enrol in astrology classes themselves. Many astrologers will set up a chart for the moment of the consultation and relate that to the client's chart. The chart reading itself then becomes a catalyst for change.

If an individual has reached a certain crisis or emergency (as in 'emerging'), the astrologer, unaware of this person's inner psychological state, will often intuitively and synchronistically focus on the appropriate astrological configurations and illuminate the larger cosmic picture.

I was fortunate to observe a most striking example of this. A businesswoman came to have her chart read and as is my custom I taped the session for her. A few weeks later another woman, Clare Martin, came to have her chart read. When asked how she heard about me, she said that she ran her own office-management business, which involved amongst other things typing letters, writing reports and making transcripts from tapes. 'I was transcribing this tape of one of your chart readings and whilst listening I was saying over and over again that I wanted this too.' After her reading, not only did she waste no time in joining the world's best astrology school, the Faculty of Astrological Studies, but also became one of their tutors and is now Vice President! In that 90-minute session her life changed so totally that it also affected the rest of her family in a most positive and profound way. Needless to say, on the day of her first reading she signed the death warrant of her business.

It was a chance glance at the chart of a client's son that brought about the realization of another vocation. My client mentioned in a therapy session that her older son, then 15, was in trouble with his school, not only for playing truant but also for smoking dope. She was afraid to leave him alone in the house because on various occasions she had come back to find him surrounded by a group of friends and a huge cloud of intoxicating smoke. I could immediately see from the horoscope that this young lad had an above average potential for acting. The mother dismissed this outright. 'Ask him,' I persisted. 'He doesn't like school anyway. At least if he does something he enjoys he will keep out of trouble.' Then she wondered how she would pay for full-time drama school and who would have him anyway, etc., etc., bringing up one obstacle after another. However, she went home and put it to her son. He jumped at the idea, left his school and enrolled in drama college. Before he had finished his three-year course he landed a good part in a TV drama and has not stopped working since. Now, several years later, he has carved out a brilliant and lucrative career for himself. This is only one example of what can happen when an astrologer looks at a birthchart. But the real synchronicity lies in the right timing of the event. A year earlier the reading might have been too soon and a year later it might have come too late.

Synchronistically, as I am writing this chapter on astrology, Uranus, the astrologer's planet, is passing right over my birth Moon. Had I planned the writing of the various chapters of this book astrologically, I could not have chosen a better time!

I think the planets *are* channels for energy from the Otherworld. There is no doubt in my mind that they are living entities. They are named after ancient gods and curiously embody their characteristics. They act as transmitters of archetypal forces. Some planets, when they visit or pass over key points on our birthchart, exert a beneficial and ordering effect on our lives, others act as a destructive force, bringing one cycle of our lives to an end before a new one commences.

The synchronicity in planetary visitations lies in the fact that when they occur, the time for necessary alteration of the working pattern of our lives has come. We don't necessarily experience these interventions as a welcome visit – we are more likely to fear the imminent changes and try and ward them off! But trying to stop this development, which was in any case encoded in our souls from before birth, is like trying to stop the clock to save time. The greatest gift we can give to ourselves is to cease being afraid of the future and to look out for the promise of synchronicities to guide us instead.

Our dreams, visions, reveries, snippets of songs and astrological transits are all signposts on our mysterious, if at times perilous, journey through life. In all these pointers, large and small, the hidden other is at work, pulling us this way and that until we find our feet firmly planted on our destined path. If an opportunity presents itself which we are in danger of ignoring, there is a creative force out there that will be on the lookout for us. It will often come uncalled, but if we acknowledge it, we will attract it and its accompanying benevolent influences in greater abundance, and it can change our lives.

THE GAMBLING BOY GOD

CHAPTER NINE

Chance favours only the prepared mind.

LOUIS PASTEUR

At the beginning of life we are dealt a hand of cards and how we play this hand will determine to a large extent the unfolding of our destiny. Marie-Louise von Franz recounts in *Number and Time* that Einstein once proclaimed to the physicist Niels Bohrs that God does not play dice. The Greek philosopher, Heraclitus, on the other hand, believed that God is a boy who plays a board game: 'Eternity is a child who plays, placing the counters here and there. To the child belongs the cosmic mastery.'[1] This prompted von Franz to write that the universal energy 'is in the hands of a gambling boy god, a boy god who just gambles on a board game with this energy'.[2]

'Dice-throwing,' she goes on, 'is a very ancient symbol, used in earlier times to illustrate the creative activity of the deity.' Even Krishna, she writes, says of himself, 'I am a game of dice. I am seated in the heart of beings. I am the beginning, the middle and the end of all beings.' She also reminds us that 'the old Jews had a divination oracle in their sanctuaries in Jerusalem, and on certain occasions when the priest wanted to consult Yahweh he tried through such oracles to discover the will of God'.[3]

The archetype of play is present in both chance and synchronicity. If we take a gamble we will invoke the great player of the universe, but we have no idea whether we will win or lose. What is far more important when taking our chances is to allow whatever *wants* to happen. Loss often is a blessing in disguise, just as gain can be a curse. That is the gamble we take each time we place our bets and roll the dice.

The use of dice, bones, cards, runes and other devices in order to discern what the universe has planned for us has always been a part of cultural life. Most divinatory techniques will delineate the bigger picture and give us an answer that relates to what should happen in accordance with Fate's plans. This is why it is sometimes so difficult to understand an oracle: we do not fathom its message because it has a far deeper and more comprehensive meaning than an answer to a straightforward question.

Likewise, when we ask an oracle about a certain life situation its answer will not reveal precisely what will happen in the future. But when the moment arrives and we understand the message, we are often amazed and amused by the uniqueness and ingenuity with which the fates have woven together a unique assortment of threads to make a completely new pattern – and they do it by the quickest and most energy-saving route possible, if we let them. Some of the synchronicities described in this book seem so far-fetched that they are hard to believe. But that is precisely the point. When Fate steps in, miracles are possible and circumstances will contrive to bring something about in a unique creative act. That is the nature of synchronicity.

Each synchronistic phenomenon is a gift from the goddess Dike. She held a special place among the ancient Greek deities. Dike was the way of the world, the way of nature, the way things happen, synonymous with the Chinese idea of *Tao*. She ruled over the rising and setting of the stars, the phases of the moon (the moon was sometimes even addressed as Dike), and she guarded the courses of the sun and the whole cosmos.[4] She was one of the three *horai*, which means 'correct moment'. The horai are goddesses of the 'right order to live by'. They bring things to ripeness, to the right moment. Their rule kept order amongst the gods, between gods and men, and especially between the two sexes.

Dike means 'Just Retribution' and her sisters were Eunomia, 'Lawful Order', and Eirene, 'Peace'. These were the gifts that the daughters of Themis and Zeus brought to the world. Dike's wheel moved through time, controlling the seasons and ensuring that everything assumed its rightful place. But when mankind transgressed her laws she became an avenging deity. She eventually became so disgusted with man's abuse of natural law and order that she invented the dice, threw them among mortals and told them to get on with it and take their chances. She then disappeared, never to be seen again, and life became little more than a precarious gamble.

We have been gambling ever since; it is part of our nature. The very act of incarnation is a gamble, begetting children is a gamble, living through every day is a gamble, trying to stay out of trouble is a gamble. It would appear that there is no such thing as playing it safe. We don't know if or when we might be struck down with an illness or meet with a terrible accident. There are no guarantees in life and no certainties except death.

Depending on our motivation, trying to take a peek at the future can be either a good or bad thing. If we simply use divination in order to see whether we will win the lottery or meet the right partner, but are unwilling to change our present, then the oracle will tell us nothing. If someone asks for a Tarot card reading and only wants to know about the future without being willing to look at the wider picture, the reading will do them no good. In fact, I would not read the cards for someone at all unless I had first read their horoscope or I already knew them well enough. Just waiting passively for good fortune to fly in through the window, without lending Fate a hand, is a waste of time. As with gambling in casinos, we need to place a bet; we need to offer something in return for a possible win. The saying 'You get out of life as much as you put into it' is a cliché, but true nevertheless.

Whilst the game of dice gives everyone an equal chance, the ancient Chinese oracle of the *I Ching* tells us how to *increase* our chances. Jung wrote:

> I had known for a long time that there were intuitive and 'mantic' methods which start with the psychic factor, and that take the existence of synchronicity as self-evident. I therefore turned my attention first of all to the intuitive technique of grasping the whole situation which is so characteristic of China, namely the *I Ching* or Book of Changes.[5]

The *I Ching* is one of man's earliest attempts to see himself as part of the cosmos and therefore subject to universal law. It eventually became one of the five classical texts of Confucianism and informed much of what we know as Taoist philosophy. The book has been used as an oracle in China for more than 3,000 years, but it is more than a way of gaining information about the outcome of a certain question. When we consult the *I Ching* about a situation in our lives it will put our question in the context of the larger picture: the circumstances that surround our present life. It is based on the premise that the universe is constantly shifting and changing and that no situation will remain the same. It counsels us to be constantly alert to these changes and adjust our characters and attitudes as the situation requires.

Many people complain that they cannot understand what the *I Ching* is saying, but that is because they don't consider the larger picture it addresses with each question. The *I Ching* needs to be contemplated, like a dream whose meaning escapes us at first. In time, as we absorb more of its philosophy, its cosmic rather than personal viewpoint, we will find the words of wisdom easier to comprehend.

The book consists of 64 hexagrams, each corresponding to a particular life situation. Each hexagram is divided into six 'lines', which suggest the specific actions that need to be taken in that particular situation in order to correct it. To access the oracle, one needs to carefully formulate a question in one's head and then either throw three coins (any coins with two different sides will do) six times or use yarrow stalks. I only use the coin method, which is very simple.

If you want to consult the *I Ching* you must first obtain a copy of an *I Ching* book, which will not be difficult as there are many on the market. I personally prefer the translation by Richard Wilhelm, as it gives you the wider picture to your question. Many modern versions are too specific, which defeats the whole object of the exercise, but they are perhaps easier to start with if you are not familiar with the symbolic language of the classic text.[6]

Most books tell you how to use the coins, but the art of consulting the *I Ching* lies in the formulation of the question. It is no use asking a question to which the answer is supposed to be 'yes' or 'no'. The question must allow for a wider answer. For instance, if you want to know whether a relationship will be good for you or not, you can ask something like, 'What is the nature of our relationship?' or 'How do I best handle this relationship?' The book will tell you, but it may take you a while to figure it out. The *I Ching* has quite a sense of humour, too.

Sometimes I only need to read the *first line* of a hexagram and have to laugh, because I am told in no uncertain terms the most obvious step I must take next. Other times the answer is so obscure that one needs to ask several times before one understands.

Sometimes it is extremely difficult to decide on a course of action, especially when one is under pressure to make a decision by a certain time. Our trust in Fate can get a little shaky then. I once asked the *I Ching* whether I should take my young son to America, where I was going to be working for a month, because I didn't know what else to do with him during the summer holidays. Someone had mentioned a Quaker camp in Vermont, but this meant an awful lot of making arrangements and flying around in aeroplanes. The hexagram I got was the Smiling Lake, which is a metaphor for pure joy. Its image is two lakes, one resting on top of another, so that the waters never dry up. The camp I had been considering was called Timber Lake and was positioned on the shores of two lakes which flowed into one another! Once I had my answer I knew I had to book our trip. My son had a wonderful adventure in this beautiful nature reserve and a couple of exciting days in New York into the bargain.

When we throw the coins they fall here and there, they might fall off the table, or spin or jump, but whichever way they fall, they will do precisely as they please, as if they had a will of their own. We cannot control how they fall. But – and this is the most important point – in that moment when we throw them, we can only do it in *that particular way*. If we try and interfere with it, this becomes part of the bigger picture, which the *I Ching* then counsels us about. The way the coins fall is completely synchronistic. It is not chance, but synchronicity, because we have thrown the coins with a particular question in mind. Gradually, if we give it due attention, the meaning might become clear, or perhaps something will happen that suddenly makes us realize what it's all about.

Consulting the *I Ching* works best when we are truly in earnest, when we have a burning question of importance, and when there is a certain amount of emotional intensity present as well. Over the years I have come to regard the *I Ching* as my wise teacher who is always available and ready to be guide and comfort. There have been many confusing times in my life when I could have despaired, or at least would have been extremely anxious for much longer than necessary, had it not been for the *I Ching*. I am sure that without it I would have made many a wrong decision.

Although one should not consult the *I Ching* over trivial matters, I have asked it about such things as changing my car. This sounds like a very superficial thing to do, but at the time I had a very small car and was given the opportunity to buy a much larger one. The price was very reasonable, but I was deeply worried about the extra running costs involved. So I asked the *I Ching*. The answer made me laugh: 'The small departs and the great approaches.' Shortly after my purchase my son was accepted at a boarding school near Glastonbury, in Somerset, a near four-hour drive from London. The new car was a hatchback and the boot was just big enough to hold the large trunk he needed. My little car would have been totally useless for the journey and as his school was in the middle of the countryside, it would not have been practical to take the train. In some uncanny way, something 'other' already knew that I needed a bigger car, not only by synchronistically presenting me with the opportunity to purchase one, but also by telling me clearly that it was in my *Tao* to let the 'great' approach. There was a whole history behind my son finally gaining a place in this particular school and the new car which was to take him there perfectly completed a vital chapter.

One can ask the *I Ching* almost anything one wants, provided one is prepared to accept the answer. If you are being trivial and are treating the oracle as a parlour game, then it will warn you clearly not to ask such silly questions. On the other hand, if you are in earnest and the question is important to you (although it might seem trivial to someone else), it will give you a deeper insight into the workings of Fate than you had bargained for. This questioning is one of the best examples of synchronicity in action.

One of the extra benefits from consulting the *I Ching* oracle is that it also has a relatively calming effect. When we are in a very difficult situation and the *I Ching* tells us that great good fortune is on its way, we can stop worrying and continue with our usual round of daily duties. But watch out for synchronicities, keep your eyes and ears open, and wait upon the will of heaven...

Whilst the *I Ching* is mainly a personal tool for inner development and a source of wise counsel, there is another type of divinatory technique that is suitable as a means for helping others make more sense of their lives and that is the Tarot, or 'the royal path' as it is sometimes called. As with the *I Ching*, synchronicity is deeply interwoven with the underlying order that makes an accurate reading of the cards possible. First they are cut in a certain way and then shuffled. The cards will arrange themselves the only way possible in that very moment. That is the synchronicity. The shuffling of the cards is synchronized with a specific moment in time. When I then place the cards on the table in order to read them, I don't look merely at a collection of images; on the contrary, what I see before me is a coherent and ordered pattern. I don't read the cards 'psychically' but literally. Each card has a specific meaning and the way they order themselves during the client's shuffling makes perfect sense to me.

As with the *I Ching*, the cards also look at the wider picture, but rather more specifically. Many a time have I seen a marriage, divorce, good fortune, promotion or emigration before the client had an inkling of the impending changes. In one situation I told a wife that she would get her longed-for separation, but saw in the husband's cards a happy marriage. How was I to square this? In the event each got what they wanted. Yes, they separated, but living apart turned out to be a huge success and they became lovers all over again, without ever resuming the former marital life.

The first time I had my Tarot read I could barely shuffle the cards. My right arm, including most of my hand, was in plaster after a nasty fall and I was very drowsy from painkillers.

I didn't think that my sparse shuffling would work and that the cards would give an accurate reading. I was also sceptical about anything as 'tacky' as a Tarot reading. Mary Wynn, the most intuitive and sensitive card reader I have ever had the honour to meet, and who later became a good friend, also thought that it needed more mixing of the cards than I was capable of. But what followed was a most amazing and life-changing reading. I had been absolutely terrified of the Tarot up to that day, because of the Death card. I thought that if it turned up for me it would be a very bad omen. And it did turn up, and many other 'nasties'. Mary quite accurately depicted the state of my marriage and the difficulties I still had to face, but also that eventually there would be a divorce and another marriage. She even described my future husband and the fact that we would be doing a great deal of travelling together. She also informed me that I had a great talent for reading the Tarot and that I should learn to do so.

At this low point in my life this reading could not have been timed better. I cheered up almost immediately, bought a deck of cards on the way home and set about learning how to read them that same night. I did have a rather difficult time ahead of me; in fact there were years still to go – years in which I developed my craft as an astrologer and Tarot card reader – before the next stage of my life could commence and I could finally meet Ean, who had been so accurately described by Mary. And we have done a great deal of travelling together and still do.

In the right hands, the Tarot is a wonderful tool for self-discovery and for gaining a glimpse of the Otherworld. I have often wondered about the future that these strange cards inevitably reveal. People frequently ask how the cards work. We don't know is the simple answer. Because they come under the law of synchronicity, which is an *acausal* connecting principle, we can find no rational explanation. All we know is that the cards can depict events long before they become apparent. Does this mean that they already exist in some other dimension? How else could we know about them in advance? My personal view on this is that the various divinatory methods let us partake for a brief moment in a reality that belongs to the mind at large and time eternal.

My introduction to the Tarot cards completely erased any fear of the future. The Death card is no longer an image of horror, instead it is an indication that one cycle must come to an end before a new one can begin, for in order for there to be new growth in the spring, the tree must shed its leaves. Similarly, we need to let go of many things throughout life in order to make room for the new.

How we use the coins or the cards is the question. The words we choose when we interpret them and the type of advice we offer is the key to whether we regard foreknowledge as a gift from the gods or only use it as a means of gaining power and prestige. Synchronicities are announcements, messages and reminders from a divine source in the Otherworld, a world that is nevertheless part of the same world in which we live and move and have our being, and as such they deserve to be treated with great respect.

NOTES

1 Marie-Louise von Franz, *On Divination and Synchronicity*, Inner City Books, 1980.

2 Ibid.

3 Ibid.

4 C. Kerenyi, *The Gods of the Greeks*, Thames & Hudson, 1979.

5 C. G. Jung, *Synchronicity*, Routledge & Kegan Paul, 1955.

6 I use mainly the following three books for reference:

a) Richard Wilhelm, *The I Ching*, Routledge & Kegan Paul, 1951.

b) Stephen Karcher, *How to Use the I Ching*, Element Books, 1997.

c) Sarah Dening, *The Everyday I Ching*, Simon & Schuster, 1995.

THE KISS OF AN ANGEL

CHAPTER TEN

These holy spirits and princes of heaven are always present with us, and assist us in all our actions.

St Alphonsus Liguori

Angels also have a part to play in synchronicity. Angelic beings have been known for as long as we have been able to perceive of the notion of God, but today more and more people are establishing a conscious connection to them. Angelic messages, hints, nudges and interventions are of the nature of synchronicity because they come at the right time, when we least expect them and when they are most needed. Jung regarded angels as 'personified transmitters of unconscious contents which announce that they want to speak',[1] whilst many people believe, when visited by an angel, that it is God in person who wants to make contact. If angels are transmitters of energies from the divine, then perhaps in some way they could be regarded as emanations from God.

On many occasions, during a Rebirthing session for instance,[2] people have claimed to be in the presence of God or angels. Such an encounter always has a profound effect and frequently changes a person's spiritual outlook fundamentally. One woman, who was very sceptical but at the same time also deeply religious, reluctantly came for a Rebirthing session and within minutes of reaching an altered state of awareness found herself in the presence of a whole choir of angels. They surrounded her for approximately 30 minutes and accompanied her to lofty heights where she experienced an extraordinary state of grace and bliss.

During these sessions encounters with angels are not uncommon, but, sadly, some people dismiss them as *only* visions or figments of their imagination, even though the experience was as real to them as any other, and frequently more real, in that it was more intense than ordinary consciousness.

As messengers, angels act as transmitters of knowledge between two worlds; they stand at their very threshold. That is why during a near-death experience people almost always encounter an angel in the form of a benign presence. If one's time to go to the beyond has not yet arrived, they will gently point back towards Earth, otherwise they will guide the soul safely to the next stage of its journey. At least this is what has been reported by psychics who are in regular communication with inner guides.

One such guardian of the threshold is the archangel St Michael, with his sword and the scales with which he weighs the souls. In Celtic mythology he is a guardian of the Underworld. Wherever he is worshipped, or where there is evidence of a strong association with a particular location, there is an entrance to the Otherworld. Only those who have earned the right may enter.

The divine presence of an angel can be experienced in many different ways. You may sense it in the room where you have been sitting in quiet contemplation; you may hear a delicate sound in one of your ears, usually the left, which rings on and on, to distinguish it from other sounds of that kind; you may feel a gentle touch on your shoulder, like the delicate brush of an angel's wing, to reassure you. Some people, in moments of deep peace or great distress, will perceive of a being of light; others will have the sensation of warmth slowly spreading throughout their bodies. Occasionally an angel will announce himself audibly. The one thing all these encounters have in common is a feeling of protection and benevolence.

When an angelic being brings a message we accept it without question, for the experience is so numinous, so altogether different from ordinary life, that we immediately *know* that we are in the presence of some higher authority. The information angels transmit for our benefit is not accessible to us via normal channels of communication. As in all incidences of synchronicity, communication becomes possible when a gap in the separating veil appears, allowing us to partake for a brief moment of a transcendent reality that is otherwise unreachable. What we are told, however we perceive it, is exactly what we need to know, there is no arguing with it and no choice. It is almost like a command. Sometimes the message makes us laugh because it is so obvious. Why couldn't we have thought of it ourselves?

I was once in deep meditation at a point in my life when nothing seemed to be going right. I felt trapped in an extremely difficult situation and was concentrating intently on trying to hear an answer to my dilemma, or at least receive some kind of guidance, when out of the blue I got my answer. The voice was that of an old man and it came with a German accent and a hint of humour, such as you might hear in a German war movie: 'Ve are showing you ze best vay how!' This made me laugh because it made so much sense and I never worried about that problem again, knowing that I was not alone, that someone on the other side was watching and doing what they could.

Amanda, a busy mother in her thirties, was regularly visited by an angelic being during a time of great difficulty, when each day was as challenging as the next, but she needed to keep her inner turmoil to herself because of her two small children. She was often aware during the night, when she awoke for no reason, of a presence standing by her bed. Sometimes it was a figure dressed in blue and sometimes in silver grey. It was always surrounded by a light hue and would stand perfectly still and exude a sense of peace and love. She knew then that all would eventually be well.

To know that we are not alone, that each one of us has a guardian angel, is a great blessing. Fortunately, we are living in an age, the Age of Aquarius (which is often depicted by an angel), when the link to the angels is once more being forged consciously and deliberately, from both sides of the veil.

If things take longer to improve than we think they should, it is worth remembering that patience is an angelic quality and when we are waiting upon the will of heaven with patience, matters can fall into place more easily. If, on the other hand, we keep complaining that in spite of doing all we can nothing seems to be happening, we are blocking the channels of communication with our bad moods, pessimism and often even criticism of Fate itself. We may be doing all we can in terms of toiling and fretting, but are we patiently creating the right environment for Fate to step in, for an angelic being to intervene on our behalf? It seems that agitated demands do not attract angels and neither does self-pity. If you want more angelic energy in your life you must prepare your environment accordingly, both physically and mentally. Candles, incense, soft music and colours all invoke the presence of otherworldly beings, as do prayer and meditation. Angels are interested in the quest we undertake here on Earth in order to further the soul's evolution. Therefore, the more we open our hearts, the more we strive for purity of intent and purpose, and act *as if* we were already divine beings ourselves, the more likely it is that we will hear an angel's message.

A few years ago I read an account of an event that happened to a couple of quiet middle-class elderly ladies. They were driving through the desert on their way somewhere. This was something they didn't usually do and they were therefore probably less prepared for mishaps than they should have been.

In the middle of the desert highway they had a puncture. They got out to examine the car but had no idea how to fix it. Then from out of nowhere a white shiny car pulled up behind them. Two men in white suits got out and silently set about changing the tyre. When they had finished they got back into their car, sped off at lightning speed and disappeared into thin air.

As well as looking after elderly ladies, angels are particularly interested in protecting children from harm. Children are forever getting into dangerous situations and often when they are involved in a car accident, they miraculously escape uninjured. When my husband was still a baby and could not yet walk, he was sitting on his mother's bedroom floor one day playing whilst she was reading the morning papers in her high four-poster bed. Suddenly he appeared on the bed next to her, as if placed there by unseen hands, only seconds before a large piece of plaster came away from the ceiling and crashed down where he had been sitting. One could say that he was saved in the nick of time when an angelic arm stretched down and lifted him to safety. J. G. Bennett calls this gap in the dividing wall *hyparxis* – that 'moment of conscious experience, without because', when eternity, space and time are one; when forces converge and opposites come together.

Angels know more than we do. They know when we are likely to be in danger and if we are sensitive enough we can hear their warning. At other times they literally intervene to prevent disaster. Angels are not subject to the laws of what we know as time and space, and they are not limited by the imprisoning constraints of matter.

Angels also make appearances in our dreams. They may come in the guise of a wise person, an animal, a voice, a knowing child, a prince or, indeed, as a winged being. The messages and the knowledge they attempt to impart are of vital importance to our present life situation. Often they bring the news that a difficult situation is about to come to an end or that someone is in trouble and needs our help. Sometimes they warn us of terrible danger.

One young woman, whilst on a solo trip through Nicaragua, nearly met her Maker one night after she ignored a voice in a dream that said, 'Don't go with the silent ones' (also known as the dead). The next day she turned down an offer to spend the night with a Danish family who were worried about her safety and had warned her that the village she was determined to reach was known for its sinister atmosphere and strange happenings. She disregarded the warning and continued on her own. It was around midnight when she reached her destination and booked into a shabby hotel. That night she escaped death only by locking herself in her room and pretending not to be there in order to keep out a violent madman. The next morning she heard that someone else had been murdered instead. She didn't hang around to find out who but got out of the place as fast as possible.

Unfortunately we are rarely prepared for visits from the other side. We wonder and ponder and talk about the numinosity of an event, but we rarely act immediately. I missed one such opportunity a few days ago whilst in London with my husband. We were walking back from a restaurant late at night across Battersea Bridge. A tall man in his thirties, with a greyish pale face and shoulder-length blond hair, wearing a dark suit, stopped when we passed him and said, 'Hey, are you folks alright?' My husband took a step back in alarm and replied, 'Yes, perfectly.' I turned round and watched him walk away, and then, without reflection, remarked, 'That was an angel!'

But, alas, it is with hindsight that we can put it all together and understand. I so wish now that I had asked him what he meant, because at 4.30 the next morning Ean was rushed to hospital in an ambulance and was put on oxygen and intravenous steroids. For some unknown reason he had developed breathing problems and was in danger of suffocating. It was touch and go for a while and we both thought that he would die that night. Had I not been so surprised by the grey-faced man's approach, I probably would have engaged him in conversation. But as so often, this was a case of encountering an angel unawares.

We can assume, however, that we always have a silent audience that watches over us and listens to our thoughts and particularly to our intentions. As soon as we are ready for the next move and the time is right, the necessary assistance will be forthcoming. It may not always be the kind of help that we want. Angels cannot interfere in our soul's evolution, but they can smooth the path and give us a nudge here and there to make us more conscious and enable us to make our own decisions and find our way.

One way is through angel cards. A card, containing a single word of encouragement, is drawn each day. This may seem a little too simplistic for the more sophisticated and mentally polarized individual, but those who have drawn angel cards and tried to apply the principle throughout the day have been astonished at the number of synchronistic occurrences that arise in connection with that one word.

Angels are playful; they can be like innocent children, full of lightness and fun. Likewise, we may ourselves be respected when we work, but we are loved when we sing and play. Angels are best approached and thought of in this light-hearted way. If we make hard work of it and get too serious, they stay away. In order to be in touch with angels we need to attune our consciousness to a lighter vibration than we are normally used to. This is why angelic beings can best communicate with us when we are either asleep, in deep meditation or in another slightly altered state of consciousness. Some people find that when they are physically occupied, as when they are gardening, cleaning or knitting for instance, they get a sense that a presence is nearby watching. Occasionally someone will feel a gentle brush against their clothing – just an angelic nudge.

There is a painting by the nineteenth-century French artist William Adolphe Bouguereau entitled *Spring*. Spring here is a beautiful young woman surrounded by fluttering putti playfully teasing her into life. In another of Bouguereau's paintings, *Work Interrupted*, we see a playful putto mischievously sitting on a young girl's shoulder, tickling her cheek with a straw. She looks around, interrupting for a brief magical moment her work at the spinning wheel, wondering what it is that is touching her. The little angel is clearly in love with her and delighted that he managed to get her attention. In *Invading Cupid's*

Realm, we see a semi-naked provocative young woman surrounded by a delightful and mischievous group of putti. They seem to be thoroughly enjoying their uninvited guest and she appears to be welcoming their advances with great joy. Whether the painter had this in mind or not is unclear, but in any case what he captured with great beauty and sensitivity is the sensuality, pleasure and playfulness of angelic paradise.

One way of raising our vibratory rate is simply by smiling. Try it out right now. Just smile for a few seconds and notice what happens to your body. Then frown and slump and imagine you are depressed. Now smile again and imagine that you are surrounded by little angelic beings that are trying to entice you to play with them. Do you feel the difference in every cell of your body? Now think of what I have just suggested as nonsense and register how your body reacts to your thoughts. Now switch back to smiling and imagine a magical scene of innocence and happiness. Again, notice how your body responds to these light-hearted thoughts and images.

In his illuminating book *Quantum Healing*, Deepak Chopra tells us that happy thoughts produce cancer-fighting cells. In other words, when we are happy, or have happy thoughts, our body's immune system is boosted, but when we are miserable, critical or sceptical, the opposite happens. When our bodies function at a higher and lighter frequency we are permitting light to enter it to a far greater extent than if we harbour dull and unhappy thoughts. When we smile, especially when we smile inwardly at ourselves, it is as if we are giving ourselves a massage of light and love on the inside. If like does indeed attract like, then this inner lightness of being really will attract angelic presences. In any case there is something to be said for simply *feeling* lighter and happier.

Another way of changing our vibratory frequency is through breathing in certain rhythmic ways. In my book *Rebirthing: Freedom from your Past* I explain in detail how to breathe the Rebirthing way, which is a method of entering safely into an altered state of consciousness and an angelic realm. If practised regularly, this particular type of breath could become the way you breathe quite naturally, and you could keep your body's frequency at a higher than average level all the time. This would not only make you more sensitive to other people's thoughts and feelings, but also to the presences of angelic beings, inner guides and visions, intuitive insights and synchronicities. Once we have forged a conscious connection with the Otherworld we need never feel alone again. All it needs is a willingness on our part to suspend disbelief and engage with our waiting and eager helpers.

NOTES

1 C. G. Jung, *Von den Wurzeln des Bewusstsein*, Rascher, 1954.

2 *See* Deike Begg, *Rebirthing: Freedom from your Past*, Thorsons, 1999.

SOUL MATES

CHAPTER ELEVEN

When two people have come into touch with each other,
without any doubt, they have something in common.
How should a bird fly except with its own kind?

RUMI

For the majority of people it is relationships that make the world go round. Without intimacy, without someone special in our lives, we may well ask what is the point of it all? No amount of money, power or status can make up for the benefits that an intimate relationship brings. Why else, when we meet the 'right' person, are we suddenly carried off to lofty heights? Why else are we disturbed, restless, sleepless, even beside ourselves and out of our minds, when we fall in love? When we walk in the rain with the beloved we sing and dance, and each precious drop turns to gold.

Love at first sight is a synchronistic event which occurs when the moment is right, even if the two people need to wait before practical matters can fall into place. They may meet on a flight across the Atlantic but live in different countries, they may both be married to other people, one of them might just be off on a round-the-world trip or finishing a PhD in the Amazonian rainforest. The stories that I have come to hear of how people first met are often quite bizarre. It would appear that Fate has sometimes gone to amazing length to orchestrate the coming together. And if at first we don't notice the flirting, the jerk or the blow, Eros, the god of love, will shoot a few more arrows until we do.

Accounts of people knowing in an instant that the other person would become their partner in marriage are more frequent than one would at first imagine. When my friend Anita returned with her five children to the USA after living in London for several years, she was at a low point in her life. She had been badly let down by a man whom she had thought of as her soul mate. Soon after her arrival she went to the funeral of an old friend. When her eyes met those of the widower on the other side of the crowded room, she knew there and then that she was looking at her future husband. He also confided in me one day that he, too, had the same thought. They have been happily married now for almost 20 years.

I first met my husband Ean in a dream in which I was in France taking a bath with a man. We were singing Hoagy Carmichael songs together and I felt very happy. Some months after this dream I briefly saw this man I was to marry more than ten years later. I was at a lecture and he sat across the room from me. We looked at each other for the whole evening. I was with my friend Charles Harvey at the time, who must have noticed our fascination and pointed out that I was looking at Ean Begg, as if I was supposed to know the name. When we walked out at the end of the lecture, as if by serendipity, I found myself walking right behind him and felt a bizarre buzzing throughout my whole body. The next time I saw him was on a television screen a few years later. He was being interviewed and I felt most odd because there was something familiar about the face and I thought that I ought to know this man. It was not until I saw his name coming up at the end of the programme that I remembered. We had a couple more encounters, but again, only from a distance. It was almost exactly four years after our first 'meeting' that we became lovers. It all started in Lucerne, in Switzerland, and that first night we finally ended up in a bath together, singing Hoagy Carmichael songs! Ean told me that he had painted a picture of me more than ten years earlier, when I had come to him in a dream.

Our story, romantic as it is, is not unusual. If two people are destined to meet, if they are *meant* to come together, love will find a way and it does so by means of synchronicity. Almost daily I hear of bizarre synchronicities where Fate throws two people together. Maybe we have an unconscious, subliminal steering mechanism that knows more than we do and skilfully guides us this way and that until we find the right partner. Or maybe we are indeed watched over by a guardian angel, a guide or a spirit of some kind, that knows better than us what we need. And then there is astrology. It is not difficult for a trained astrologer to predict the times when we are most likely to meet a future partner. Astrologically speaking, such things as the beginnings of new relationships are blatantly obvious.

It is my belief that the less we interfere with the ways of Fate in matters of relationship, the more easily the future will unfold. Ean and I had to wait another five years before our circumstances favoured a more permanent union. At the beginning of our relationship there were no indications at all that this would be more than a fine romance. But we continued in spite of strong contra-indications. Neither of us had plans for a future together, but neither of us had plans for a future without the other. Fate had dealt us a hand of cards and we played it.

In the early days, when we were seeing each other without any future expectations, we visited my friend Carol, who lived in another part of London. We had never been there together before and when we passed a church whose portals were open we went inside to have a look. The church was decorated magnificently with sweet-smelling flowers in preparation for a wedding. As we walked down the aisle the organ suddenly started up, loud and enthusiastically, with the 'Wedding March' from Wagner's opera *Lohengrin*. I knew in that instant that this was a sign that no matter how difficult our individual lives were at the time, one day we would be married. From that day our relationship took on a different *feel*. But it was not for another ten years that the promise of that coincidence would be fulfilled.

At some level we are all interdependent and the desire to share our life with someone else is natural. Whether we are any good at intimate relationships depends a great deal on our upbringing, education and personal characteristics. Some people are scared of intimacy and either avoid it altogether or ensure that an intimate union has only a limited lifespan. As soon as it gets too cosy they are off. But the fact that they keep on looking is an indication that perhaps they *are* seeking more than a kiss and a promise after all.

In the end it is better to be in a relationship than not. Even if it seems to be going nowhere, it can be used to practise on. If you know that a certain relationship is only for the moment, that the other person is not committed and never will be, you have nothing to lose. Although you may not be emotionally ready at this stage to give this relationship a miss, you can use it as an opportunity to ask for what you want, even if you haven't a chance in hell of getting it, and to learn to say 'No' to things you feel are offensive. You can tell the other person what you don't like about them and, above all, you can learn to become more independent. You are unlikely to encounter many synchronicities with such a person, but what you can learn will be useful for future relationships.

But relationships that have a deeper meaning tend to attract synchronicities in large numbers. And it is not only at the beginning of meaningful relationships that odd and significant things happen. Christina, an attractive and capable Scotswoman, came to consult me in Glasgow because she was not happy with her marriage. It was the second time round for both partners and they had several children between them. She wanted to know what to do about her husband's ex-wife, who seemed to be telephoning him so often that she found it invasive and wearying. She wanted the other woman to *back off*, but her husband, Greg, felt obliged to talk to her. I was sympathetic, knowing that such a situation can be extremely difficult. Although there is no real threat to a relationship in such a case, a partner can feel under pressure just the same.

That evening Christina called me and said that she had something to report which I ought to put on record for future reference. After she had left my house she had had a synchronistic experience. She was driving down a one-way street when a large saloon car came towards her the wrong way. And who should be driving it but her husband's ex-wife, who now had to *back off* all the way up the narrow street. Christina felt that this meant that the tide was now turning for her, that things would change, and they did.

The other thing that worried Christina was that the ex-wife was still wearing her wedding ring and she didn't feel that this was right. She had been married to Greg for many years and felt that the adjustment period ought to be over by now. Then something happened which made her feel that she wasn't being selfish after all in wanting less of the ex-wife's influence in their lives and that Fate was taking a hand in things. Greg's former wife had three cats and one day one of them went missing. A couple of days later someone telephoned to report that her cat had been spotted in a garden near the main road. When she went to collect it, she found it under a bush, petrified. As she went to pick it up it attacked her and deeply scratched her left hand in several places. The wound festered and she needed medical attention. Her fingers had swelled up so badly as a result that the doctor had to cut off her wedding ring to allow for better blood circulation. Needless to say the ring stayed off henceforth.

A further synchronicity concerned a watercolour painting Greg kept in his office at work. The picture was of a cottage in Wales that he and his first wife used to stay in at weekends. Christina felt uncomfortable about it and wanted it removed. Greg refused. But synchronicity will find a way. Shortly after the cat incident, the picture came crashing down from the wall and the glass shattered into a thousand pieces. Both Christina and Greg were instantly aware of the significance and Greg did not bother to have the painting reframed.

It is often when we experience intense emotional distress that synchronistic happenings come to the rescue. When the Theosophist Alice Bailey was absolutely destitute with three small children to feed, she went to the little hill near her home and threw herself on the ground in despair. The following morning she found a box of groceries on her doorstep. A family that was also destitute sat together one night and prayed to God for help. Before they could finish the prayer there was a knock at the door. It was a stranger who had passed their house and had fallen in love with their antique wrought-iron gate. He offered them a handsome sum of money for it. When Saint Theresa of Lisieux had been sick for a long time and feared that she would no longer be able to carry out God's work, she prayed with such intensity that she was healed soon afterwards.

In all these examples a call for help was heard and answered. Who hears and who answers? During such synchronistic moments, with the aid of the power of emotions, we penetrate the veil that separates us from the Otherworld and are able to reach a magical power that can bring solace, practical help and healing. Maybe we really do live in only *one world* and at certain crucial points in our lives cross over into another dimension, just as we cross from a waking to a sleeping state and back again. And emotional intensity, particularly in love relationships, attracts synchronicities.

A light-hearted and amusing example is what happened to Carl, a businessman in his early forties, when he went to an antiques sale in London. The only reason he went was because a friend who was over from Paris had asked him to. Whilst there, Carl was strangely attracted to a woman on the other side of the room and couldn't take his eyes off her for the whole duration of the sale. Afterwards he left the salesroom with his friend and flew to Madrid for a conference. He kept thinking about this woman and couldn't get her out of his mind. He was meant to fly on to Geneva for a meeting early the following morning, but at the last minute that was cancelled. He decided to stay over in Madrid and visit the Prado museum instead. After dinner he went for a stroll and just as he was turning into the main square he literally bumped into the woman he had been mesmerized by in the London salesroom. They got talking and a couple of years later are still talking and married.

Love can make the most extraordinary things happen in the physical world around us. When two people are destined to be together nothing in the world can keep them apart. Circumstances will arrange matters in such a way that their union becomes possible.

This happened to Mariella, who was married to Stan, a dangerous individual. She never knew what mood he might be in from one moment to the next. He could be violent, loving, depressed or joyful, sometimes all within a measure of minutes. Stan is what might be termed a social psychopath. Mariella stayed with him only because of their four children and an unsatisfactory financial situation.

Alexander was also married with responsibilities. When he met Mariella it seemed that they were in an impossible situation. No one in their right mind could have given their liaison any chance. But the two were so much in love and spent as much time as they could together, although initially without any sexual involvement, as they had nowhere to go apart from coffee bars and restaurants. There were no signs that things might change at any time in the future and the pair accepted the limitations of their relationship without regret and without expectation of an improvement. But then Mariella finally divorced Stan, though he still wouldn't leave the family home, and within a year Alexander's wife divorced him. He was now free against all the odds, but Stan refused to budge and kept on making threats.

Mariella didn't know how to progress. Then she had a dream in which her husband had been particularly violent and was threatening to smash up the home. She called the police. As they arrived he ran out into the garden and turned into a rotten apple that finally merged with the earth. She had the dream three times within one week.

Shortly after this Stan stopped coming home. Mariella found out that he had been involved in a motorcycle accident and killed someone, and that he had gone back to live with his mother for comfort and support. He had been drinking heavily that day and the crash had clearly been his fault. He was sentenced to 18 months in gaol. From that day neither Mariella nor her children ever saw him again. She and Alexander took this as a sign that they had a future together after all.

The great German genius Goethe believed that the soul possesses magical powers which can make things happen in the physical world. In his book *Synchronicity* Jung talks about the connection that exists between emotional intensity and synchronicity, and quotes from a text by St Albertus Magnus, the medieval theologian and Doctor of the Church (*c.*1200–1280). In conclusion I think it is worth repeating Jung's quote in full:

> **I discovered an instructive account [of magic] in Avicenna's *Liber sextus naturalium*, which says that a certain power to alter things indwells in the human soul and subordinates the other things to her, particularly when she is swept into a great excess of love or hate or the like. When therefore the soul of a man falls into a great excess of any passion, it can be proved by experiment that it (the excess) binds things (magically) and alters them in the way it wants, and for a long time I did not believe it, but after I had read the nigromantic books and others of the kind on**

signs and magic, I found that the emotionality of the human soul is the chief cause of all these things, whether because, on account of her great emotion, she alters her bodily substance and the other things towards which she strives, or because, on account of her dignity, the other, lower things are subject to her, or because the appropriate hour or astrological situation or another power coincides with so inordinate an emotion, and we (in consequence) believe that what this power does is then done by the soul... Whoever would learn the secret of doing or undoing these things must know that everyone can influence everything magically if he falls into a great excess ... and he must do it at that hour when the excess befalls him, and operate with the things which the soul prescribes. For the soul is then so desirous of the matter she would accomplish that of her own accord she seizes the more significant and better astrological hour which also rules over the things suited to that matter... Thus it is the soul who desires a thing more intensely, who makes things more effective and more like what comes forth... Such is the manner of production with everything the soul intensely desires. Everything she does with that aim in view possesses motive power and efficacy for what the soul desires.[1]

NOTES

1 C. G. Jung, *Synchronicity: An Acausal Connecting Principle*, Routledge & Kegan Paul, 1955.

Hold on to the Great Image
and all under heaven will approach you.
Coming to you and not being harmed,
they will find rest, peace, and security.

THE TAO

SELECTED BIBLIOGRAPHY

Adrienne, C., *The Purpose of your Life*, Thorsons, 1998

Allenby, A. I., *Angels as Archetypes*, Spring Publications, 1963

Assagioli, R., *Psychosynthesis*, Turnstone Books, 1975

—, *The Act of Will*, Wildwood House, 1974

Begg, E., *Myth and Today's Consciousness*, Coventure, 1984

—, *The Cult of the Black Virgin*, revised and expanded edition, Arkana, 1996

Begg, E. and D., *On the Trail of Merlin*, The Aquarian Press, 1991

—, *In Search of the Holy Grail and the Precious Blood*, Thorsons, 1995

Begg, D., *Rebirthing: Freedom from your Past*, Thorsons, 1999

Bennett, J. G., *The Dramatic Universe*, vol.II, Hodder & Stoughton, 1961

Cameron, J., *The Artist's Way*, Pan, 1994

Dening, S., *The Everyday I Ching*, Simon & Schuster, 1995

Franz, M.-L. von, *Number and Time*, Rider, 1974

—, *C. G. Jung: His Myth in our Time*, Hodder & Stoughton, 1975

—, *On Divination and Synchronicity*, Inner City Books, 1980

—, *Psyche and Matter*, Shambhala, 1992

Harrison, J., *Themis*, Merlin Press, 1963

Hyde, M., *Jung and Astrology*, Thorsons, 1992

Jaffé, A., *The Myth of Meaning*, G. P. Putnam's Sons, 1971

—, *Apparitions*, Spring Publications, 1978

Jung, C. G., *Synchronicity: An Acausal Connecting Principle*, Routledge & Kegan Paul, 1955

—, *Letters 3/33*, Routledge & Kegan Paul, 1955

—, *Mysterium Coniuntionis*, Routledge & Kegan Paul, 1963

Karcher, S., *How to Use the I Ching*, Element Books, 1997

Kerenyi, C., *The Gods of the Greeks*, Thames & Hudson, 1979

Mansfield, V., *Synchronicity, Science, and Soul-Making*, Open Court, 1995

Marciniak, B., *Bringer of the Dawn: Teachings from the Pleiadians*, Bear & Co., 1992

Mares, Théun, *The Mists of Dragon Lore*, Lionheart, 1998

Parker, D. and J., *The Complete Astrologer*, Mitchell Beazley, 1971

Rumi, *Daylight*, Threshold Books, 1994

Sheldrake, R., *Dogs That Know When Their Owners Are Coming Home*, Hutchinson, 1999

The Tao: The Sacred Way of Lao Tzu, ed. Tolbert McCarroll, Crossroads, 1982

White, R., *Working with Guides and Angels*, Piatkus Books, 1996

Wilhelm, R., *The I Ching*, Routledge & Kegan Paul, 1951